Neue Deutsche Welle

Forthcoming in the series:

Neue Deutsche Welle

Claudia Lonkin

BLOOMSBURY ACADEMIC
NEW YORK · LONDON · OXFORD · NEW DELHI · SYDNEY

BLOOMSBURY ACADEMIC
Bloomsbury Publishing Inc
1385 Broadway, New York, NY 10018, USA
50 Bedford Square, London, WC1B 3DP, UK
29 Earlsfort Terrace, Dublin 2, Ireland

BLOOMSBURY, BLOOMSBURY ACADEMIC and the Diana logo are
trademarks of Bloomsbury Publishing Plc

First published in the United States of America 2024

Bloomsbury Publishing Inc does not have any control over, or
responsibility for, any third-party websites referred to or in this book. All
internet addresses given in this book were correct at the time of going
to press. The author and publisher regret any inconvenience caused if
addresses have changed or sites have ceased to exist, but can accept no
responsibility for any such changes.

Whilst every effort has been made to locate copyright holders
the publishers would be grateful to hear from any person(s)
not here acknowledged.

A catalog record for this book is available from the Library of Congress.

ISBN: PB: 979-8-7651-0333-3
ePDF: 979-8-7651-0335-7
eBook: 979-8-7651-0334-0

Series: Genre: A 33 1/3 Series

Typeset by Deanta Global Publishing Services, Chennai, India
Printed and bound in Great Britain

To find out more about our authors and books visit www.bloomsbury.com
and sign up for our newsletters.

Contents

Introduction: Translating the New Wave

If the twentieth century was the century of the subculture, then the twenty-first may prove to be the century of the microtrend. After the Second World War, the emergence of a new middle class in the West was accompanied by the rise of an all-encompassing monoculture. Giving allowance for regional variations, the ascendant middle class of Europe and North America valued consumer consumption, private property, and the nuclear family. However, this lifestyle was not for everyone. Whether by choice or because they were excluded from new visions of postwar prosperity by dint of their sexuality, race, or differing ability, many people sought alternatives. Often, these people came together to form small, but strong, communities of like-minded individuals. Over time, these communities became subcultures: mods, punks, rude boys. These subcultural communities are lasting, significant phenomena, with attendant aesthetic markers and nuanced politics.

The microtrend, conversely, is not thought to have the same politically subversive character. Seen inherently as a product of algorithm-based social media, microtrends (e.g., vaporwave, cottagecore, or doomerism) inform patterns of consumption, not politics. Nor do they have an immutable effect on one's identity. One can switch between, splice, or try on microtrends, simply by accessorizing with the right clothes or listening to the right music. But are the politics of an e-girl any different from those of a dark academic? A core critique of the microtrend is its short shelf life, which makes the construction of meaningful communities difficult, if not impossible. The necessity of consumption as a means of participating in microtrends in some ways makes the concept inherently reactionary, ensuring that it ultimately works to uphold the capitalist status quo.

A dichotomy begins to emerge between the subculture and the microtrend. Subcultures are politically charged and oppositional to the mainstream. Microtrends uphold established patterns of consumption. Subcultures are lasting, microtrends are ephemeral. Subcultures are, as a historical phenomenon, rooted in the postwar twentieth century. Microtrends are a product of the commercialized internet and social media in the twenty-first century.

This conceptualization is too neat by far. In the early 1980s, a cultural phenomenon emerged that has many of the trappings of both a subculture *and* a microtrend: the music genre, neue deutsche Welle (NDW). Neue deutsche Welle emerged at the very tail end of the 1970s in the Federal Republic of Germany (FRG), colloquially referred to as West Germany. The name "neue deutsche Welle" literally translates to "German new wave." NDW music was not simply British- or American-style new wave, sung in the German language. It developed its own vernacular, symbols, and, indeed, had a unique historical trajectory. It resembles a subculture, in that it provided an alternative way of life and cultural sensibility for a new generation of Germans who felt that the postwar vision of success in their country was exclusionary, repressive, or otherwise false. Indeed, neue deutsche Welle often functioned as a subversive challenge to the status quo. At the same time, the genre presaged the microtrend in many ways. It had a vanishingly short life span; the prime years of the genre are considered to be 1981 to 1984—less than half a decade. The trappings (often represented through clothes, makeup, or hairstyles) of neue deutsche Welle were quickly adopted and abandoned by artists and music consumers alike.

The supposed rivalry between the independent, meaningful underground versus the superficial, commercial mainstream has dominated much of the historiography surrounding neue deutsche Welle. The historian Christian Jäger argues that there are two stages of NDW, the first being more artistic and experimental, followed by a commercial phase that sought to exploit the sonic stylings of NDW for profit.[1] One music journalist dubbed this first phase "original neue deutsche Welle," advocating a split terminology.[2] The common narrative is that NDW began as an independent, countercultural movement against consumerism, wealth inequality, and political ignorance but was co-opted by the mainstream cultural apparatus, which appropriated its fashions and sounds and used them to pump out a glut of radio-friendly pop music.

---

[1] Christian Jäger, "Ripples on a Bath of Steel—The Two Stages of Neue Deutsche Welle (NDW)," in *German Pop Music: A Companion*, ed. Uwe Schütte, 131–50 (Berlin: De Gruyter, 2017).
[2] Klaus Walter, "A Guide to Neue Deutsche Welle," *Red Bull Music Academy*, September 3, 2013, https://daily.redbullmusicacademy.com/2013/09/neue -deutsche-welle-feature.

It was this turn, from the independent to the massive, which is said to have spelled the end for neue deutsche Welle.

This book will challenge that narrative on several levels. First, it will put the genre in context, of both the broader, global post-punk and new wave musical scene and the domestic story of the postwar period in German-speaking countries. While new wave music came to West Germany from Britain, the particular way in which it was adapted to the specific national context reveals crucial differences between the experience of British and German youth in the postwar era. This is especially important, because so much of the existing literature on post-punk and new wave music concerns the British (mostly English) and American (mostly New York) scenes. Indeed, there are many similarities here too, which can tell us a great deal about the ongoing movement toward political and cultural globalization. However, neue deutsche Welle needs to be examined as an independent phenomenon. While the terminology is in some sense transferable from English-language scenes, the German "new wave," in fact, encapsulates a lot of music that might more properly be considered post-punk. In that sense already, "neue deutsche Welle" is both a more flexible term and one that could be used to, in turn, reveal the complexities of the English-language scene. Likewise, many of the postwar economic conditions that produced post-punk and new wave music were heightened in West Germany. The process of postwar reconstruction was all the more dramatic, given that the infrastructure of the country had been heavily damaged (and, in some areas, outright destroyed) during the war. The legacy of Nazism only heightened intergenerational tensions between the older set, who had fought in the Second

World War, and the youth demographic that gave birth to neue deutsche Welle.

The second chapter of the book will begin to discuss the notion of the "two sides" of neue deutsche Welle, by examining, first, the earlier, underground scene, discussing at length the broader political, as well as specific local, context that shaped the NDW sound. The West German scene should not be written about as a monolith; there are several important cities with distinctive cultural symbols and musical sounds. The role of the city itself, as the simultaneous center of postwar prosperity and urban decline, is also crucial. Special attention will be paid to the role of women and gay people in the underground, as well as the intertwined nature of the neue deutsche Welle scene and the West German contemporary art community. Such activities are evidence that NDW was a broader subculture, part of a network of independent cultural producers and creatives that not only provided a superficial identity but also articulated an alternate mode of life.

From there, the book will pause to engage in a greater discussion of the Cold War political context. This historical background explains how the supposed duality of neue deutsche Welle is more accurately described as a porous exchange between the genre's two constituent sounds. Groups like ALU on the songs "Solidarnosç" ("Solidarity") and "Scheiss DDR" ("Fucking GDR"), Brausepöter on "Bundeswehr," Geier Sturzflug on "Besuchen Sie Europa" ("Visit Europe"), Gleitzeit on "Ich komme aus der DDR" ("I Come from the GDR"), and Lilli Berlin on "Ostberlin - Wahnsinn" ("East Berlin - Insanity") make reference to the politics of the time. Much like the Cold War, the NDW scene was portrayed in popular culture as strictly divided, with little to no crossover between two oppositional sides. In reality, both the Iron Curtain and the internal genre boundaries of NDW were permeable and often imagined. Metaphorical similarities aside, the Cold War itself (especially the Space Race) influenced the work of many neue deutsche Welle musicians. First among them must be the NDW stars of the German Democratic Republic (GDR), commonly referred to as East Germany. The stereotypical understanding of East Germany (and, indeed, any Cold War, Communist state) is that culture was heavily regulated, the only messages that art was allowed to convey were those approved by the state, and any hint of Western culture—rockstars, Coca-Cola, and blue jeans—was to be stringently repressed. There is some truth to this gross oversimplification. All aboveground culture (because there was an independent underground) was produced under the auspices of the state. The East German government had a monopoly on cultural production. Volkseigene Betriebe (VEBs, or "Publicly Owned Enterprises," essentially state-run companies) controlled the process of musical recording, record pressing, and touring. However, censorship was often less hands-on and explicit than is thought to be the case. Instead, the state created an all-encompassing culture of political conformity that precluded the possibility of any rogue actors rising through the ranks of the artistic apparatus. That is not to say that all East Germans were forbidden from listening to any song with an electric guitar or a drum machine—much the opposite. The East German government actually embraced neue deutsche Welle when it emerged in the West and later sought to produce their own version of the genre, which was both very similar and yet fundamentally distinct from the NDW created by private artists in capitalist West Germany.

On the subject of the role of capital in cultural production, the fourth chapter will return to the question of the "two sides" of neue deutsche Welle, this time to consider the more commercial half of the equation. The overall aim of this chapter is to show that while there are two separate subgenres of NDW, in terms of both the economics of cultural production and the sound of the music itself, they operate more as two ends of one spectrum, rather than diametrically opposed poles. This chapter will consider the intersections between political awareness, creative innovation, and pop music. While there are many examples of mindless commercial neue deutsche Welle, there are just as many artists who used the audio stylings of pop and dance music to create politically aware hits. Most prevalent was a third type of musician, who either created NDW music of varying quality or crossed over between the independent and mainstream scenes. This chapter will also discuss the institutional apparatus that underpinned the commercial neue deutsche Welle scene, which, again, was not so different from, and often overlapped with, the networks and institutions of the independent scene.

Next, though the main focus of this book is West Germany, it is important to discuss the neue deutsche Welle music that was created outside the political borders of the FRG. East German NDW was a feature of Chapter 3, but at this time there were four large German-speaking states, and all of them had their own musical scenes. The bulk of this chapter is devoted to the Austrian scene and more specifically to the artist Falco. Falco is an outsize figure not just in Austria (whose broader historical and cultural context is embedded in his work at every possible level) but indeed across the international neue deutsche Welle scene and even the German music of today. In addition, the Swiss scene, which in many ways was closer to Great Britain than it was to the FRG, is a focus of this chapter. Most important is the discussion devoted to racial minorities in neue deutsche Welle. One can observe several racist trends in NDW music: orientalism, the romanticization of the mythical "noble savage," and the appropriation of Black culture. In this sense, neue deutsche Welle is not just a product of its time. It is a reflection of West German postwar anxieties regarding the decline of the colonial world order, the leading role Germans had played in the genocide of Jewish and Roma peoples during the Second World War, and the global rise of the appropriation of African-American culture. In this context, appropriation refers to the adoption of the speech patterns, music, and fashion of African Americans by non-Black creatives, without acknowledging the genealogy of these ideas, in a manner that very intentionally disenfranchises the original Black creators, stripping their work of context for the profit of those outside the community. It is crucial to discuss these legacies of neue deutsche Welle in order to come to terms with the genre as a whole and its representative role vis-à-vis German society.

The final chapter deals with the history of neue deutsche Welle after 1990. During the late 1980s, the genre continued as a result of inertia, with artists, both independent and commercial, continuing to try to make music in an increasingly apathetic market. Slowly, the institutions that had underpinned the community fell apart. However, if the Cold War had been the essential political context for the genre, then the "fall" of the Berlin Wall likewise signified the start of a new beginning for neue deutsche Welle. During the 1990s, many NDW artists turned to dance music, becoming part of the burgeoning neue deutsche Tanz ("new German dance") genre and the broader Eurodance movement. Even more important than the legacy of neue deutsche Welle in dance music is its afterlife as a key inspiration for the next defining genre of German popular music: Deutschrap ("German rap"). In Germany, neue deutsche Welle and Deutschrap are both cornerstones of the cultural canon and perform a similar function in society.

Although it is simultaneously both/neither, neue deutsche Welle spans the age of the subculture and the advent of the microgenre. Indeed, attempting to pin NDW down creates new ground for discursive debates surrounding cultural classification, historical periodization, and questions of authenticity. In that sense, working through the perennial questions posed by neue deutsche Welle music is a productive exercise through which one can gain new insights into not only German cultural history but also the global politics of the Cold War and how culture (even cultural movements that last less than a decade) plays a central role in society.

In summation, neue deutsche Welle is a genre of German-language popular music that broadly existed from 1979 to 1989 but was at its peak from 1981 to 1984. Equal parts avant-garde and commercial, many contemporary listeners and post-facto critics have created a false dichotomy between these two strains of neue deutsche Welle, when, in fact, they cross-pollinated frequently. The genre included minimalist and maximalist synth, post-punk guitars, and new wave drum machines, spoken, politically charged vocal dirges, and melodic songs about teenage love. Its fashions could likewise be gothic and punk or straightlaced and flashy. In every aspect, NDW was equal parts alternative and aspirational. Above all, neue deutsche Welle was informed by the broader political context of the Cold War and the unique place of German-speaking countries such as the Federal Republic of Germany, Austria, Switzerland, and even the socialist German Democratic Republic in the middle of this global conflict. These states were vulnerable but not necessarily empowered, creating a nihilistic anxiety toward the new technologies of the Cold War, especially spaceflight and the atomic bomb. This specific geopolitical anxiety only fed into broader trends in new wave music, showing how neue deutsche Welle was at once specific to the German-speaking context and part of a global movement.

Finally, a note on language and translation. All artist names and album and song titles are given first in the original German and then the English translation. Note that in the German language, all nouns are always capitalized. In titles, only the first word and nouns are capitalized. This book preserves the traditional convention in both languages, which does lead to some discrepancies. The term "neue deutsche Welle" and its abbreviation NDW are also used interchangeably, instead of using the full term on first mention and then the abbreviation on all following occurrences. This is to reinforce that the name, in the original German, would always be said in full, instead of as an acronym, even when it appears as such. Additionally, it should be made clear that as used in this book, the word "German" in "German new wave" refers to the German language, not the state of Germany. Indeed, there were two states using the name "Germany" during the 1980s and the German language was in use in Austria, Switzerland, and Liechtenstein.

1 The New Wave Travels East

New wave music is not native to Germany. It sprang from the punk scene in the UK. Punk itself originated in the 1970s as a reaction to commercialism and skillsmanship in mainstream rock music. The punk sound was raw, loud, and often angry, but most important was its cultural emphasis on the do-it-yourself attitude, which applied not only to music but to fashion and politics as well. Musical skill was de-emphasized, if not openly scorned. The rhythms, chords, lyrics, and vocals of punk music are simple, all the better to preserve its undiluted message of social alienation, exemplified by bands such as the Ramones, the Sex Pistols, and the Clash. Punks fashioned their own clothes (pins, studs, patches, intricate hairstyles, and customized items were all common), published their own zines, and released their own music through independent (or even bootleg) channels. Though punk originated in the United States and Britain, its highly accessible and personalizable nature meant that it spread around the world rapidly. This is also due to the mass appeal of punk's guiding ethos, the slogan "no future." Equal parts nihilistic and hopeful, "no future" acknowledges that society, in its current iteration, provides no future for anyone who wants to live alternatively—to reject consumerism, social conservatism, and power hierarchies—implying, however, that those on the margins can make a different future for themselves. Still, in its commitment to amateurism and rejection of anything that might be deemed mainstream, punk was singular, and such singularity invited challenge and innovation.

The rise of post-punk, then, should be no surprise. Post-punk is a difficult genre to define. While the term was used sporadically in the late 1970s, it was far from the only moniker given to new trends in popular music. "Art rock," "new musick," and even "new wave" itself were all terms that were used to refer to this burgeoning style of music, which resembled punk in its alternative spirit but incorporated a much more omnivorous and intellectual spate of influences. Taking cues from dub music, bands like Wire, Joy Division, and Gang of Four iterated on the punk sound, sharpening its political critiques and refining its amateur, do-it-yourself agenda. They drew inspiration from cultural critics such as Guy Debord (and the larger Situationist movement that he was a part of), economic theories of development, and artistic movements including Dadaism and the avant-garde.

Post-punk is mainly discernible by these new intellectual influences. Sonically and aesthetically, it is a midpoint between punk and new wave, and its musical styles and fashions overlap with those two genres a great deal. Despite this ambiguity, the term is still useful, even as a post-facto definition elucidated by critics. It indicates the plastic nature of musical subdivisions in the 1970s and 1980s, alluding to the fact that many musicians' work evolved along with genre markers. Because the post-punk trends toward musicianship and intellectualism culminated with the advent of the new wave, this terminology also provides a useful shorthand for discussing hierarchies of taste.

New wave music embraces synth(etic) artificiality. The music is both enmeshed with technology and yet still wary of it. The use of the synthesizer and drum machine is the clearest sonic hallmark of new wave music. Bands like New Order, Blondie, and Depeche Mode continued the move away from traditional musical expertise (intricate guitar solos and trained vocal performance), while developing a new proficiency in programming and electronics. The prominence of new technologies in new wave extended beyond the mere sound of the genre. A general fear of the future and dissatisfaction with modern life is an intellectual hallmark of new wave music. This attitude is reflected in the fashion of new wave, albeit in multifarious ways. Some new wave musicians adopted a bland, almost white collar manner of dressing, emphasizing their role as the operators of new musical machines (the "real" musicians). Others embraced the futurist implications of the new wave, donning bright colors and incorporating metallics and plastics into their wardrobes. These two trends indicate both the intellectualism of new wave and its turn back to more identifiably pop aesthetics. Fans of the genre point to its subtle political messages as an example of sophisticated nuance, while its detractors claim it is defanged and commercial in comparison to punk and post-punk.

As new wave traveled around the world, it changed character, though these fundamental debates would follow the genre. From its birthplace in the United Kingdom, new wave music spread first to the United States, helped along by the shared language. It wasn't long before the new wave turned east, crossing the English Channel and making landfall in continental Europe. In West Germany, music lovers could see the wave coming in the years before neue deutsche Welle came into its own. Music magazines, like the independent publication *Sounds* (of no relation to the UK music weekly of the same name, which, in fact, was started four years *after* the German magazine), published articles on new wave bands in the United Kingdom, the United States, France, and the Netherlands.[1] "New wave" sections appeared in listings of available stock advertised by record stores, but the artists were almost exclusively British or American. By the late 1970s, new wave was known, but it was fundamentally a foreign genre.

Prior to the advent of neue deutsche Welle, German popular music had been dominated by a genre called Schlager (literally "hit" or "winner"). Unlike NDW, Schlager is not a band genre and has historically been dominated by solo vocalists and even, today, DJs. Schlager music can be traditional or modern in its instrumentation. It is impossible to constrain it to any one sonic repertoire; its fundamental character has everything to do with its national, popular character. It is a kind of contemporary German folk music, always evolving, but also always German. Schlager hits have included adaptations of folk standards, euro-disco, and EDM (electronic dance music) festival bangers.

---

[1] See, for example, Willi Andresen, "Vitesse: Schnelle Jungs und flinke Schulmädchen," *Sounds*, January 1979, 19–20; Elisabeth Daniere, "Französischer Rock: Käske ssäh???" *Sounds*, February 1979, 42–4; Elisabeth Daniere, "Französischer Rock: Käske ssäh??? Teil 2 · Lyon Roque," *Sounds*, March 1979, 42–4; Elisabeth Daniere, "Französischer Rock: Käske ssäh??? Teil 3 · Punque Adieu," *Sounds*, April 1979, 28–30.

Outside the mainstream, there was also German-language punk and rock music, but neither of these genres took on a unique German character. They still sounded and functioned much as their counterparts in the United Kingdom and the United States did. This is where neue deutsche Welle is unique. It was unmistakably German, like Schlager, but arrived at its ethno-linguistic character by transforming a music genre that originated abroad, in a way that German punk and rock were unable to accomplish.

A significant amount of neue deutsche Welle's success on this front comes from its innovative use of language. As many neue deutsche Welle artists admitted themselves, the German language can be difficult to use in typical pop music.[2] In German, verbs are often pushed to the end of sentences, creating long phrases whose meaning does not resolve simply. This grammar is not well suited to pop songs with short, snappy lines that communicate simple messages. Schlager is a German-language genre, but, in many ways, it evolved out of operetta. That means that the use of German in Schlager is very formal. Schlager songs often have a more narrative format, with an emphasis on storytelling and a preservation of long phrases in lyrics. When faced with the question of how to adapt the German language to foreign popular music forms, German rock bands frequently chose to avoid the problem. Their songs are often instrumental (especially in the case

[2] Alfred Hilsberg, "Neue deutsche Welle: Aus grauer Städte Mauern," Sounds, October 1979, 20–5; Alfred Hilsberg "Aus grauer Städte Mauern (Teil 2): Dicke Titten und Avantgarde," Sounds, November 1979, 22–5; Alfred Hilsberg, "Aus grauer Städte Mauern (Teil 3): Macher? Macht? Moneten?" Sounds, December 1979, 45–8.

of prog and psychedelic rock), and if they did sing, it was in English. One prominent example of this phenomenon is the experimental band Can.

Conversely, German punk music was more frequently sung (or rather, shouted) in German, as befits its more prescient political messages. Punk lyrics in German are about as graceful as their English-language counterparts. That is, not very. The point of punk is to deliver raw emotions, not nuance, so poetic innovation was not required to create effective German-language punk.

Neue deutsche Welle is more subtle. The genre's lyricists were the first to manipulate the quirks of the German language to enhance their songwriting, instead of trying to work around them. They used German's modular nature to create complex rhyme schemes and played up elements like "split" verbs (in which a key meaning-denoting prefix is split off from its verb and sent to the end of a sentence) to subvert typical linguistic stress patterns and create surprise meaning. They also modified words and bent grammatical rules when it suited them, evolving the language by ignoring word-order rules and dropping verb endings to achieve the ideal number of syllables in a given line. It is this linguistic innovation, in part, that makes neue deutsche Welle such a defining part of postwar German culture.

At the turn of the 1980s, the new wave reached West Germany. British and American bands like the Clash and Talking Heads were already popular, but now, domestic acts were putting their own spin on the genre. Coverage of English-language bands did not stop just because of the rise of neue deutsche Welle. Groups like New Order, Wire, and Echo and the Bunnymen remained popular. In fact, only three German musicians or bands were featured on the cover of *Sounds* throughout its foreshortened 1980s run (the monthly magazine went out of business after its January 1983 issue): Hans-a-Plast, Deutsch Amerikanische Freundschaft (DAF), and Palais Schaumburg. The rest of the cover stars were British or American. Still, it was impossible to turn back the tide. Neue deutsche Welle was here, and it was not just new wave in translation.

Postwar German Youth Culture

Aside from foreign music genres, neue deutsche Welle was influenced by postwar German youth culture. After being the main aggressor and perpetrator of genocide in the Second World War, Germany spent the rest of the 1940s rebuilding, both literally and in terms of economic potential. The state was remarkably successful in this endeavor, and in the 1950s entered the era of the Wirtschaftswunder, known in English as the German economic miracle; one NDW band even named themselves after this phenomenon. This recovery was in large part supported by the United States under the auspices of the Marshall Plan, which provided economic aid to European states, including West Germany, and indicated a broader willingness on the part of Western powers to rehabilitate the German national image in order to position the FRG as a reliable, capitalist partner against socialist East Germany and its Cold War ally, the Soviet Union.

This decision to prioritize economic recovery over political reckoning would have consequences. In the 1960s, young

Germans became concerned about the presence of former Nazis in government, business, and other powerful positions in society. They believed that their parents had neglected to confront their own roles in the Holocaust and hold their country accountable. A major catalyst for the youth movement was the 1962 *Spiegel* affair, when journalists from the leading German political magazine *der Spiegel* ("*The Mirror*") were arrested and charged with treason, and the publication's offices were raided, all because they had been reporting on the postwar rearmament of West Germany. From there, New Left and antiestablishment ideas only became more popular among young Germans, largely because they felt they had no voice within traditional institutions of power. From 1966 until 1969, West Germany was governed by a grand coalition of the center-left Social Democratic Party and the center-right Christian Democratic Union, which controlled 90 percent of seats in the country's legislative house, the Bundestag, during this period. Those with beliefs even slightly outside the mainstream were not represented in government at all. On top of that, the press was dominated by right-wing tabloids owned by the media mogul Axel Springer, which spread misinformation and stoked anti-left violence. If young people outside the mainstream wanted to be heard, they would have to find other ways, outside of politics and the press, to express their opinions. Thus, the Außerparlamentarische Opposition (APO, or "Extra-Parliamentary Opposition") was born.

The APO was just one part of the larger student movement in West Germany and around the world. Unsurprisingly, its members were against the Vietnam War and the new mode of middle-class consumerism that was becoming the idealized way of life throughout the West. The movement's most prominent member was Rudi Dutschke, a sociology student and activist who garnered much public sympathy after a failed assassination attempt by a right-wing reactionary, who was himself inspired by the 1968 assassination of Martin Luther King Jr.

The assassination attempt on Dutschke, for all that it engendered sympathy for the student activists, also created a rift in the German youth movement that would grow throughout the 1970s. While Dutschke himself advocated for a strategy of change from within, in which activists would strive to find places in existing institutions of power and then attempt to reform them internally, other activists became radicalized by the assassination and came to the conclusion that the only way to fight violence was with more violence. An assortment of left-wing terrorist groups sprung up in West Germany (and throughout Europe and the United States) during this time, but the most prominent was the Rote Armee Fraktion (RAF, or "Red Army Faction"), also known as the Baader-Meinhof Group. The RAF was responsible for a number of kidnappings, assassinations, and bombings. The height of their activities was fall 1977, a period known as "German Autumn," after which the core members of the group were apprehended and died under disputed circumstances in a maximum-security prison.

This was the stage, then, onto which neue deutsche Welle emerged at the very end of the 1970s. Since the end of the Second World War, German youth culture had occupied an antiestablishment place in society, but it was now at an inflection point. Some young Germans turned to violence, radically rejecting mainstream society and attempting to destroy it in order to create their vision of the future. Others, newly empowered by their activism, sought to enter the institutions of power they had previously seen as inaccessible and attempt to reform them from within. Most importantly, it was cool to be political. Organizing was not just a tool for change but also an opportunity for socialization. On one hand, this attitude encouraged people to become more knowledgeable about the forces that governed their lives. However, it also had negative consequences. When politics becomes cool, brands begin to use the aesthetics of activism in order to sell their products. This problem is particularly acute among those companies that attempt to seduce consumers by creating a vision of a "lifestyle" to sell to them.

This problem of authentic "coolness" versus contrived commercialism would come to plague neue deutsche Welle. For every band expressing their opinions in a fresh, sonically innovative way, there was a group adopting the hallmarks of political engagement or skimming the musical signposts and popular fashions of neue deutsche Welle to make hits. Neue deutsche Welle was a popular genre and that means that plenty of genre-hopping bands saw that the wave was cresting and took advantage of it. For every band that protested the lack of economic prospects for young people, the pressure (especially on women and gay people) to conform in society, or the fear of nuclear annihilation in the ongoing Cold War, there was another band that appropriated the working-class struggle as superficial set-dressing, used female vocals to add an "edgy" twist to their otherwise-mainstream music, or played with Cold War politics while ultimately not trying to challenge the status quo.

Differences Between New Wave and NDW

In order to examine this duality, we have to explore the meaning of neue deutsche Welle in greater detail. Neue deutsche Welle literally translates to "German new wave," but the genre is not a one-to-one analog to British or American new wave. As mentioned earlier, in English speaking countries, there is a more delineated transition from punk, to post-punk, to new wave. While there is German punk, there is no clearly defined German *post*-punk; both music that sounds like post-punk and music that sounds like new wave are grouped together under the neue deutsche Welle banner.

At first listen, it is tempting to say that this sonic dichotomy correlates with the authenticity divide discussed earlier. After all, in Britain and the United States, the move from post-punk to new wave signified a move away from political substance and toward a more commercial-friendly sound. However, that transition occurred over a much longer time line; post-punk and new wave dominated much of the 1970s and 1980s sound in English-speaking music markets. Neue deutsche Welle operated on a far more compressed timetable. It did not become a phenomenon until 1980, was at its zenith a year later, and was considered played out and passé by 1984. All told, its life span was about a quarter of its counterparts across the English Channel and the Atlantic. Instead of having time to evolve in a more linear fashion from post-punk to new wave, neue deutsche Welle saw the contemporaneous presence of sonic stylings from *both* these genres. Even if neue deutsche Welle had had time to develop distinct post-punk and new wave phases, ascribing a varying degree of authenticity to these genre subdivisions is problematic. While it is generally true that new wave music is more ripe for commercialization, this is not true in all cases. Some post-punk music is very contrived, and some new wave music challenges the status quo.

Neue deutsche Welle is notorious for having a deep well of commercial, trend-chasing bands. Artists like Spider Murphy Gang and Münchener Freiheit, who practically took up residence on the *ZDF-Hitparade*, a countdown chart show produced by Zweites Deutsches Fernsehen (the second public television channel in Germany), are classic examples of new wave commerciality. They rely on pop-y, upbeat synth hooks, frequently sing about being young and having fun at parties (see, for example, Purple Schulz's 1985 hit "Verliebte Jungs" ("Lads in Love")), or otherwise write songs with gimmicky lyrics, chosen for the ease with which they could be sung along with or because of their memorable absurdity, not for any deeper meaning. For example, when the band Combo Colossale's 1982 song "Puppen weinen nicht" ("Dolls Don't Cry"), which could perhaps be understood as a lyrical parody of the Cure's 1979 song "Boys Don't Cry," was performed by the band on the *ZDF-Hitparade*, lead singer Michael Flexig literally serenaded a children's doll. Die Conditors' 1984 hit "Himbeereis im heissen Tee" ("Raspberry Ice Cream in Hot Tea") features an absurd, attention-grabbing title, and lyrically the majority of the song is about a picture-perfect trip to America, including a stop in Disneyland. This strategy was even mocked (coincidentally, two years earlier, using the same flavor) by the band Bizarre Leidenschaft on their 1982 song "Himbeerschokoladentorte"

("Raspberry Chocolate Cake"), which also uses the repetition of a childish word. However, because of its minimalistic production and amateur vocals, the song comes across as a satire of everyday life and the ultimate emptiness of life's little pleasures, such as cake, smoking, or sex.

However, plenty of artists within neue deutsche Welle were able to use the new wave sound in a compelling, politically incisive way. The biggest neue deutsche Welle hit of all time, Nena's 1983 song "99 Luftballons" ("99 Balloons") has an upbeat synth riff, features an obtrusive ska breakdown, and makes use of an arguably childish metaphor. Nonetheless, all these factors work in service of the song's heartfelt antiwar message.

In the same manner that new wave tropes in neue deutsche Welle could be both commercial and authentic (to the extent that those two concepts are even oppositional), so too could post-punk sounds. Experimental, boundary-pushing bands like Einstürzende Neubauten, Malaria!, and Palais Schaumburg used industrial sounds and sparse synthesizers to complement lyrics about postindustrial decline, the anxieties of life during the Cold War, and the struggles of being a young person, forced to choose between mainstream conformity and destitution. Just as the sonic tropes of new wave could be appropriated, so too could those of post-punk. Plenty of bands with nothing new to say used the sparse production, spoken lyrics, and themes of youth discontent to churn out post-punk neue deutsche Welle that sounded nearly identical to many of their predecessors. Often, these bands' songs are sexist, complaining about women or objectifying them, or expressing an entitlement to sex. They can also be racially insensitive, dealing in orientalist tropes in particular, if not outright racist, making use of the "n-word" or appropriating the struggles of Indigenous peoples in the Americas.

It would be inaccurate to attribute the decline in the "quality" of neue deutsche Welle to a shift from post-punk to new wave influences. Upbeat, highly produced pop songs often conveyed incisive political messages, while plenty of lo-fi artists released derivative industrial and cold wave music on independent labels. The "independent market," if anything, picked up pace at the same time as commercial NDW was booming. The July 1981 issue of *Sounds* describes the singles market in particular as producing new releases "almost daily" to the point that they were nearly impossible to keep up with.[3] The turn in neue deutsche Welle must be attributed to something else. The majority of this book is dedicated to examining the two sides of the genre. Its aim is to recast NDW's polarity by bringing clarity to the process by which culturally significant music was created.

It would also be inaccurate to consider neue deutsche Welle as purely a part of the new wave movement. Though its name translates to "German new wave," it contains a large contingent of post-punk and experimental bands. Because of the compressed timeline of the genre's development, these sounds overlapped, instead of building off one another, creating a unique environment of sonic diversity. Aside from the language and German cultural particularities, this is a key factor that sets NDW apart from the British and American new wave that inspired it. Art rock, no wave, and synth-powered dance tracks coexisted under the neue deutsche Welle banner.

---

[3] Neuestes Deutschland, *Sounds*, July 1981, 10.

Finally, it is the unique cultural context that not only produced the compressed time line but also gave neue deutsche Welle the characteristics that set it apart from new wave music. West Germany's changing position in the postwar cultural pipeline saw it moving closer to America and Britain, rapidly reestablishing a musical conversation in such a fashion that bands needed to play catch-up, integrating the influences of several genres at once. However, the desire to push back against the domination of Cold War powers, especially the United States, drove German artists to make neue deutsche Welle a discrete entity from Western post-punk or new wave. Its language, lifecycle, and politics are unique.

But if neue deutsche Welle isn't new wave, what is it? Is it even possible to define one of the most varied musical genres of the postwar era? These questions are not new. One of the most remarkable things about neue deutsche Welle is that debates about its characteristics, life cycle, and values are endemic to the very genesis of the genre. They don't come from present-day music critics or historians, seeking to reevaluate the genre with the benefit of hindsight. These debates have been around since the birth of neue deutsche Welle. Some NDW artists engaged in them through song. For example, the lyrics of Piefke und Pafke und die Jungs aus der Dunkelkammer's 1982 single ". . . und es geht ab" (". . . And Off It Goes") argue that when it comes to neue deutsche Welle "guitar" and "problems" are "out," while "computers" and "happiness" are "in." "All the lyrics are short and concise, so that one has something to laugh about," the song continues, before name-dropping a plethora of neue deutsche Welle hits. Musicians were not the only ones who engaged in this discourse. Before NDW was fully formed, fans, musicians, and writers were debating what to call this new sound and how to define it.

These discussions, we can assume, happened anywhere that music fans gathered—bars, concerts, apartment gigs. But they are best preserved in the pages of *Sounds*, a monthly German music magazine dedicated to music outside the mainstream. Founded in 1966, *Sounds*' original purview was rock music, and the magazine covered a large number of foreign bands, mostly from Britain and the United States, in addition to the domestic German scene. In the 1970s, *Sounds* started to cover punk bands as well and became a cultural encyclopedia for antiestablishment German youth culture. It was not an industry publication but the record of a scene and of a community.

As a testament to that community, *Sounds* includes a "letters to the editors" section at the start of every issue. This is indicative of the democratic nature of the magazine. Naturally, *Sounds* had its marquee music critics, but anyone could write in and have her work featured in the magazine, at least in theory. Some of the letters featured are crude or humorous, but others contain insightful debates regarding the nature of musical fandom. One of the most long-standing debates surrounded neue deutsche Welle.

From the start, *Sounds*' decision to cover neue deutsche Welle at all was controversial, especially among fans of rock and punk. Because there had been no gradual transition from punk, to post-punk, to new wave, some punk fans saw neue deutsche Welle as a more fundamental departure from the genre they knew and loved. For example, one reporter claimed that "punk purists" viewed "ultra-avant-garde" bands like Geisterfahrer as "decadent."[4] To these listeners, NDW was commercial and pop-oriented, neither underground nor challenging to the status quo in any meaningful way. One referenced the "punk industry," which to him included the "new" wave, in a plea to reinstate the editorial dominance of "true rockfreaks."[5] To writers like this one, neue deutsche Welle, which encapsulated both punk and new wave, was a mainstream genre in the vein of Schlager—merely an attempt to adapt popular musical forms to a superficial German context with the ultimate goal of fostering mass appeal and high record sales. For this reason, many letter-writers wanted *Sounds* to stop covering neue deutsche Welle altogether. They viewed the genre as unintellectual, a trend pushed by marketers seeking to tap into youth culture, rather than a more holistic lifestyle, like punk was often considered to be. Debates surrounding the authenticity of neue deutsche Welle, and whether the genre was a genuine subculture or merely a passing fad, are not post-facto conversations imposed by cultural critics or historians. This is not to say that they were not contrived or superficial, but they followed the scene from its early days and were of concern to everyday fans.

Many wrote in to *Sounds* arguing for continued coverage of neue deutsche Welle. To these fans, conversely, the genre was a natural outgrowth of the punk attitude. They acknowledged that many of the NDW songs were more radio-friendly but embraced the danceability and catchy hooks so often used

---

[4] Dies & Das, *Sounds*, August 1979, 6.
[5] Bernd Mehl, Leserbriefe, *Sounds*, January 1980, 4.

by the genre, and pointed out that many experimental bands were working within it as well. Interestingly, in these early letters, there is no effort to split the genre into high- and low-brow subdivisions. Its diversity is taken as a matter of course and sometimes even used to make a broader point about supposedly vaunted, established genres like punk and rock.

Beyond letters to the editors, *Sounds'* own music critics wrote extensively about neue deutsche Welle and the shifting boundaries of genre in popular music. The January 1980 issue featured an article entitled "SOUNDS *Discourse*: Ideologies, Identities, Ramblings," which poked fun at the pretensions of different groups of music enthusiasts, including "The Mellow, West Coast Party [Type]" and "The resigned, hippie intellectual," acknowledging the fault lines in the magazine's readership while encouraging them to remain open-minded toward new music.[6] These fault lines appeared to manifest in real life as well, if one *Sounds* reader, a DJ from Bremen, who wrote in to the May 1980 issue, is to be believed. He claimed that while "the scene only wants new wave, the punks only Pogo, the colored [*sic*] guys only reggae, the young girls only soft rock or Italian hits, the 30-year olds only oldies, the long-haired intellectuals only jazz-rock, the greasers only rock 'n' roll or R&B, [and] the 'beautiful young people in the styles of the new time' only disco," new wave music still comprised "more than half the music requests," and *Sounds* editors were not overstating its popularity.[7] *Sounds* itself was key to the genesis of the new

---

[6] Diedrich Diederichsen, "Ideologien, Identitäten, Irrwege?" SOUNDS Diskurs. *Sounds*, January 1980, 18–19.
[7] Ralf Behrendt, "Gesclunacksentwicklungen und Schubladen," Leserbriefe, *Sounds*, May 1980, 4. Racist language and imagery appear in *Sounds* whenever

genre. In fact, the term "neue deutsche Welle" first appeared in *Sounds*, initially in an advertisement for the West Berlin record shop Zensor, run by the producer and label-owner Burkhardt Seiler, in the August 1979 issue of the magazine and then in a three-part editorial detailing the rise of the genre, published between October and December of the same year.[8] The series is more anthropological than analytical; it attributes many of neue deutsche Welle's unique characteristics to the specific nature of postwar urban life in German cities like Hamburg, Düsseldorf, and Berlin. The integration of technology into music and the means by which musicians are able to make (or rather, not make) money feature prominently.[9] The sharp contrast caused by a development boom and the postwar economic miracle, and the fact that many young Germans remained broke and felt alienated from society, created the precise mix of tensions necessary to foster a rich cultural scene.

Postindustrial life and the uncertainties of new technologies are common features of post-punk and new wave music around the globe. In his book *Are We Not New Wave?: Modern Pop at the Turn of the 1980s*, the musicologist Theo Cateforis cites "new modern technologies," particularly those that affected household consumers in the 1970s, as the source of this new nervousness; technology "had begun infiltrating

---

people of color are discussed. Reader letters also use the "n-word," and shops selling patches, stickers, and other paraphernalia advertised products featuring the Confederate Flag and stereotypical representations of the "noble savage," a racist characterization of an Indigenous man.

[8] *Sounds*, August, 1979, 59.

[9] Hilsberg, "Neue deutsche Welle: Aus grauer Städte Mauern," 20–5; Hilsberg, "Aus grauer Städte Mauern (Teil 2): Dicke Titten und Avantgarde," 22–5; Hilsberg, "Aus grauer Städte Mauern (Teil 3): Macher? Macht? Moneten?" 45–8.

. . . everyday life," but was not yet user-friendly.[10] The feeling of being left behind by a changing economy and made obsolete by incomprehensible new devices like computers was relatable to many young people across the "developed" Western world in the 1980s.

The other main element of magazines, advertising, is also revealing. "Neue deutsche Welle" was first coined (in print at least) in an ad, and its usage in advertisements in *Sounds* continued to evolve over the years. Many record stores advertised their wares in the magazine, listing the new releases available in their shops by genre. After its initial usage, neue deutsche Welle was slow to be picked up by record stores. The more general new wave label remained popular for some time. Interestingly, the corollary label "new wave cheapos" was often used, namely in advertisements by the mail-order shop Flash. More than just a designation of a sale, this label confers a kind of inherent baseness, an association with low culture that is projected onto new wave music broadly.

Despite an initial reluctance, eventually the term "neue deutsche Welle" took off in record store advertisements. It indicated music with the new wave sound but with (predominantly) German lyrics. Though listeners could expect themes of youth discontent with politics and society, this was the essential core of the genre, but also proved to be the source of another criticism. The genre was sometimes seen as childish, relying on outlandish fashions or attention-grabbing wordplay but not backing it up with

[10]Theo Cateforis, *Are We Not New Wave?: Modern Pop at the Turn of the 1980s*, Tracking Pop (Ann Arbor: University of Michigan Press, 2011), 77.

Neue Deutsche Welle

any real substance. Add to this the fact that some of its stars, like Andreas Dorau and Markus, were quite young or did not rely on over-the-top, "macho" performances of masculinity. The (relative) lack of gendered performance was particularly irksome to rock fans, who often criticized neue deutsche Welle from a more conservative point of view than punks. While neue deutsche Welle was not a space free from gendered expectations and sexist caricatures, it was a marked improvement over the macho performance of rock music. In this sense, even though rock fans saw themselves as antiestablishment, their criticisms of NDW often carried conservative undertones.

Crucially, the presence of women as musical artists in neue deutsche Welle was not an issue for rock fans, though there were many more female artists in NDW than rock—bands like Malaria! and Liliput were entirely composed of women, not to mention the many more experimental or otherwise politically minded groups that had female members, who often were the front women. Interestingly, neue deutsche Welle attracted the most misogynistically charged ire in the instances when it was compared to disco. Americans may be familiar with Disco Demolition Night, a 1979 event coordinated by the radio shock jockey Steve Dahl that culminated in the explosion of a crate of disco records and a riot, with homophobic, racist, and sexist undertones. This rhetoric pervaded in German music scenes as well, to the point that one 1980 *Sounds* article was written as an "apology" to disco. The author begs forgiveness for writing NDW off as base, apolitical music, acknowledging its roots in Black American soul music and the Motown label, as well as the influences of disco on new wave bands like

Talking Heads and XTC.[11] Neue deutsche Welle, as a scene, was not as much a haven for oppressed people as disco was, which explains why the backlash against it was not as violent, but it nonetheless provided a forum for the criticism of mainstream society, including accepted notions of masculinity, that many found to be challenging, even disturbing.

Ultimately, the fact that fans of so many genres (new wave, punk, and rock) felt compelled to write about neue deutsche Welle reveals its eclecticism. The historical influences and social environment that gave rise to NDW were as clear to fans at the time as they are to present-day observers. What was less certain was neue deutsche Welle's future. An editorial in the July 1980 issue of *Sounds* claimed that over time, the magazine had received less hate mail from anti-NDW readers; however, the author asserted "ignorance and misunderstandings" concerning the meaning of neue deutsche Welle and the concept of new wave pervaded.[12] He concluded, pessimistically, by writing that he no longer uses the term "new wave," as it has come to represent in equal measure the creative inability to create descriptive terms for new music and the "opportunism" of trend-chasing bands, "an embarrassing attempt . . . to sell test-tube music."[13] While swearing off the genre moniker is melodramatic, the vagaries of the terms "new wave" and, by extension, "neue deutsche Welle" are not well elucidated. Philosophically, another

---

[11]Ewald Braunsteiner, "Apologie eines apolitischen Stils: Am Ende der Disco-Ära," *Sounds*, March 1980, 24–5.

[12]Thomas Buttler, "Mit 'Njuhwehf' in die Eiszeit," *Sounds*, SOUNDS Diskurs, July 1980, 26.

[13]Ibid., 27.

Sounds writer asserted that new wave is characterized by a rejection of the naturalistic individualism of rock, in favor of mechanization and a nihilistic awareness of the "cultural industry" (and the modern world more broadly) to which the individual is subordinated.[14] To understand this argument, we must establish some historical context. What exactly was NDW a successor to? Was it supposed to be a German version of American and British new wave? A development of the underground punk scene? Or a stylistic turn for guitar rock bands wanting to incorporate the synth sounds of the future? In truth, neue deutsche Welle was all of these things and more. Many of its artists were emulating foreign bands like Joy Division and Talking Heads. Others were underground, DIY art school groups, more interested in "happenings" and performance art than concerts. Some neue deutsche Welle bands, such as Bel Ami and Cats TV, were popular guitar rock groups that, in the long run, produced only one or two NDW albums before moving on to the next big trend in pop music.

Still, this book must provide some rudimentary boundaries for what it considers to be neue deutsche Welle before moving forward. The easiest element to define is chronology. While the most conservative estimates put the life span of neue deutsche Welle at only four years, from 1981 to 1984, it is not unreasonable to broaden that scope. Instead, this book proposes a longer, more politically bounded framework. Much of neue deutsche Welle is influenced by the persistent

---

[14] Josef Hoffmann, "Das moderne Ich: Ich-Strukturen und neue Musik," *Sounds*, September 1980, 22–3.

Cold War environment of the 1980s, when tensions increased and new, globalizing technologies were used for purposes of aggression, rather than peace. It makes sense to say neue deutsche Welle begins at the very end of 1979, with the introduction of the term and resultant debates over its definition in *Sounds*, but it is worthwhile to track the genre all the way to 1989 and the fall of the Berlin Wall. While it is true that the proportion of commercial acts increased over the course of the 1980s, it would take an event as monumental as the end of the Cold War and the reunification of Germany to fundamentally change the German experience such that NDW became defunct or otherwise unrecognizable.

2 Avant-Garde Beginnings

The avant-garde plays a crucial role not just in neue deutsche Welle but indeed in all post-punk and new wave music. In her 2020 monograph, the musicologist Mimi Haddon defines post-punk music as avant-garde pop music.[1] This definition is particularly useful in the context of neue deutsche Welle, because it addresses both sides of the genre: its experimental, artistic element and its fundamental mass appeal. Indeed, it is the very tension between these two aspects that often makes post-punk and new wave scenes the sites of such dramatic musical experimentation.

To be avant-garde, a work of art must simply be ahead of the curve. The term literally means "advance guard" or "vanguard" and was coined in cultural critique as early as the 1800s in France, in reference to artists who rejected the status quo of accepted aesthetic forms and values, connoting the countercultural. In neue deutsche Welle, the avant-garde manifested in several ways. Its sonic markers are the use of sparse instrumentation, often just a drum machine and synths, with either no vocals or simple, spoken lyrics. These traits

---

[1] Mimi Haddon, *What Is Post-Punk?: Genre and Identity in Avant-Garde Popular Music, 1977-82* (Ann Arbor: University of Michigan Press, 2020).

characterize the work of many avant-garde neue deutsche Welle groups, including 1. Futurologischer Congress, der Plan, and Strafe für Rebellion. Many other smaller groups worked within this experimental, at times minimalist synth sound, including Deutscher Kaiser, DIN A Testbild, Frizz, Fröhliche Eiszeit, Keine Ahnung, Knusperkeks, Liaisons Dangereuses, Mau Mau, Neue Wohnkultur, Non Toxique Lost, Notorische Reflexe, Poison Dwarfs, Roter Stern Belgrad, Saal 2, Siluetes 61, Sprung aus den Wolken, Stahlnetz, Stratis, Thorax Wach, Vono, Weltschmertz, and Z.S.K.A. Others, such as Mittagspause and Westdeutsche Christen, exemplified a lo-fi, post-punk sound. Aus Lauter Liebe, P16.D4, and die Radierer were more identifiably industrial.

At the same time, the term "avant-garde" will always retain certain opacities. In her April 1981 editorial in *Sounds*, the music critic Jill Vaudeville points out that there is nothing sacred in this terminology and that it too can be used as a marketing term.[2] While Vaudeville wants to see "a connection between avant-garde imagination and political consciousness," she acknowledges that this desire is "idealistic" and that "the authors of new music are not miraculously politically radical." Still, she deconstructs the dichotomy between kitsch—what is "easy to sell" versus avant-garde—what is "hard to sell," introducing the concept of the "mass avant-garde."[3] This understanding best encapsulates the avant-garde as it manifested in neue deutsche Welle. While culturally understood as radical and

---

[2] Jill Vaudeville, "Avantgarde? Scheissegal!" Sounds DISKURS, *Sounds*, April 1981, 30.
[3] Ibid., 31.

independent, it was often very popular and not necessarily politically radical.

By far the biggest avant-garde NDW band was Einstürzende Neubauten. Formed in West Berlin in 1980, the group pioneered the minimalist, industrial sound, often pushing the very boundaries of what was considered music by making recordings with non-instrument objects, like pieces of metal, and frequently using self-made, DIY electronics. Fittingly, their name translates to "collapsing new buildings;" the instrumental use of the cobbled-together detritus of modernity suits Einstürzende Neubauten perfectly.

We can trace Einstürzende Neubauten's influence not only through the proliferation of its sound but also through the social networks of its members. Band members were shared with, or at one time belonged to, several other important bands, including Abwärts, Mania D, and Palais Schaumburg, not to mention their solo projects, and the influence of key producers like Tommi Stumpff.

The band's name as well as their DIY, industrial sound are responses to the postwar reconstruction of Germany, as well as the later decline of industrial centers and the solid blue-collar jobs that historically kept young working-class men out of poverty. In fact, the scholar Giacomo Bottà theorizes that the postindustrial urban landscape is a common factor which unifies post-punk music across national and genre borders. In seeking to "[extend] the definition of post-punk . . . to hardcore punk, proto-techno, electronic body music, and noise experimentations," Bottà identifies "a common origin" not in shared sonic characteristics but in the common locale of "industrial towns" and the attempts therein "to respond and/

or 'dramatise' real urban crises under different geographical, social, and economic circumstances."[4] Indeed, in many ways, conditions of life in postwar Germany were not unique. Post-punk can be said to reflect the anxieties of globalization in "first world" Western countries. The music of avant-garde neue deutsche Welle artists reflects a desire to show the ugly, profoundly inequitable underbelly of the German economic miracle.

But the avant-garde did not wear all of its influences on its sleeve. The famously "empty" post-punk sound, with its deep bass, crisp highs, and sparse mids, comes from dub, a genre pioneered by Black artists in the Caribbean and imported to Europe by producers like Joy Division collaborator Martin Hannett. Haddon argues that for British musicians, borrowing from dub and reggae enabled them to generate "the symbolic capital that allows them to retroactively qualify as post-punk," recreating processes of colonial extraction.[5] Whether neue deutsche Welle artists were aware of this legacy is debatable, though *Sounds* did cover dub music at a few notable junctures.[6] Either way, it is ironic that the very process of globalization that brought avant-garde neue deutsche Welle musicians so much socioeconomic anxiety was responsible for the international cultural exchange that helped to create their distinctive sound.

[4] Giacomo Bottà, *Deindustrialisation and Popular Music: Punk and "Post-Punk" in Manchester, Düsseldorf, Torino, and Tampere* (London: Rowman & Littlefield, 2020), 13.
[5] Haddon, *What Is Post-Punk?*, 66, 63.
[6] See, for example, Kunert Reinhard, "Dub Dub Dub Dub," *Sounds*, June 1980, 36–8; Kunert Reinhard, "Dub Dub Dub Dub," *Sounds*, July 1980, 28–30.

Avant-garde neue deutsche Welle also has a distinctive set of ethno-linguistic particularities. When avant-garde musicians did employ lyrics in their songs, they were often spoken, rather than sung, and minimal. In this sense, the German language itself became a feature—vocalists exaggerated its harsh consonants and guttural dips in order to use diction as an instrument. This lends a certain rough, poetic quality to avant-garde neue deutsche Welle.

Many avant-garde bands also sang in English. Unlike commercial bands, which often started out with German lyrics and then switched to English in order to try to tap into a broader market appeal, avant-garde bands that sang in English incorporated their second language from the start. Groups like die Gesunden, Liliput, and Malaria! sang in English on early records. It is possible that this is because at the time, the neue deutsche Welle scene was in its infancy and the domestic market for this kind of music, in the German language, was unproven. Accordingly, many of these bands did enjoy international crossover: Deutsch Amerikanische Freundschaft (DAF), Einstürzende Neubauten, Foyer des Arts, Freiwillige Selbstkontrolle, Malaria!, Palais Schaumburg, die Toten Hosen, and Xmal Deutschland all were granted the honor of a Peel Session, with the legendary British radio DJ John Peel, a symbolic tastemaker of the post-punk cultural elite. Indeed, Einstürzende Neubauten continues to have a thriving international career, and Xmal Deutschland in particular was arguably more successful abroad than at home in Germany.

Domestically, postwar West Germany supported a rich web of city-based, individual scenes. In general, Germany is a regionally atomized country, insofar as it can be understood as a country at all. For centuries, Germany was the "German lands," a collection of German-speaking noble estates that were organized into various political organizations, such as the Holy Roman and Habsburg Empires, as well as Prussia. During the Cold War, the Iron Curtain produced a new regional division, with West Berlin sitting as an isolated exclave in the middle of East Germany. These historical factors gave rise to an environment in which several unique, local neue deutsche Welle scenes emerged. Though they cross-pollinated with one another, these scenes all had their own unique sounds, networks, and institutions.

The most important neue deutsche Welle city is, arguably, Hamburg. Home to ZickZack Records, the gold standard for experimental, avant-garde music, the city produced not only post-punk-style acts like Geisterfahrer and Abwärts but also new wave artists, including Andreas Dorau (occasionally referred to as the label's "enfant terrible") and Joachim Witt.[7] In addition to being a home for many foundational members of neue deutsche Welle, ZickZack was also run by one of the genre's titans, Alfred Hilsberg. Hilsberg is something of an empresario, the Tony Wilson of neue deutsche Welle, maybe, if Wilson had run *Sounds* magazine (which itself was based out of Hamburg) instead of hosting a talk show on Grenada TV. In fact, it was Hilsberg himself who popularized the term "neue deutsche Welle" in *Sounds* in his three-part feature, "Neue Deutsche Welle—Out of Gray City Walls," in which he profiled the Hamburg scene, among others. In his piece, Hilsberg emphasizes the effect that postwar industrial decline had on

[7] Neuestes Deutschland, *Sounds*, July 1981, 10.

the youth of the city, characterizing its scene as "heavier" and less intellectual and artistic.[8]

Another hot spot of neue deutsche Welle was the smaller city of Düsseldorf. Despite having less than half the population of Hamburg, Düsseldorf had a rich musical output, relative to its size, in part because of the existence of its own local, independent label, Ata Tak. Founded in 1979, in Wuppertal, Ata Tak came to represent many Düsseldorf neue deutsche Welle bands, including der Plan, SYPH, and DAF. Indeed, the label would relocate to Düsseldorf, from where it operates (albeit, in a very reduced capacity) to this day. Unlike ZickZack, Ata Tak was founded by musicians, not a journalist. It was the project of Kurt Dahlke, who performed as Pyrolator; Moritz Reichelt, a member of der Plan; and Frank Fenstermacher, an experimental musician who played on some of neue deutsche Welle's most iconic releases, including albums by DAF, Fehlfarben, and Andreas Dorau. Overall, the Düsseldorf/Ata Tak sound is similar to that of Hamburg/ZickZack. Both scenes were avant-garde and experimental, pushing the boundaries of what people considered listenable. Where Hamburg was industrial, Düsseldorf was art school. Its production was smoother, with greater emphasis on synths and drum machines than non-instruments and field recordings. This is not to suggest that Düsseldorf was less postindustrial than Hamburg—indeed Düsseldorf is one of the cities Giacomo Bottà chooses to spotlight; its sound expressed the anxieties of postindustrial life in a unique manner. A 1979 article in *Sounds* articulates

---

[8] Alfred Hilsberg, "Aus grauer Städte Mauern (Teil 3): Macher? Macht? Moneten?" 47.

the complex relationship that Düsseldorf musicians had with deindustrialization and technology. The author expresses surprise that a relatively small city could have as important a scene as exists in Hamburg, Munich, or Berlin, but stresses that there is "no other part of Germany" in which he is so struck by the "class divide" and the "importance and unimportance of money."[9] He acknowledges that if social friction does indeed increase creativity, the outstanding nature of the Düsseldorf scene should be no surprise. This author and the musicians he speaks with all stress the electronic nature of Düsseldorf's music over its industrial characteristics, while still rejecting fears that humans will become "slaves" to technology or that electronic music is substantively different than that made from "natural instruments." The author borrows the phrase "electronic lifestyles" from Kraftwerk member Ralf Hütter to encapsulate this comfort with, but awareness of, the ubiquity of technology in modern life.[10] To an extent, this mentality can be applied to the broader Ruhr area (which Düsseldorf and Wuppertal are close to but not technically part of), a historically industrial heartland. The band Deo's 1982 song "Ruhrgebiet" ("Ruhr Area") is devoted to the region, expressing a love for its industrialism, even as the lyrics acknowledge the punishing nature of the lifestyle.

Though other smaller scenes existed in Hagen, Hannover, and the Frankfurt Rhine-Main Metropolitan Region (as well as abroad, outside of West Germany—a subject that will be

---

[9] Ingeborg Schober, "Genug Energie fürs Jahr 2000: La Düsseldorfs Neu~es Kraftwerk," *Sounds*, April 1979, 41.
[10] Ibid., 43, 44.

addressed later), the third main center of neue deutsche Welle was indisputably West Berlin. Groups like Ideal, Nena, and Markus came to define the divided city's musical output. Berlin's sound is the most commercial of the "big three"—listeners can more easily find pop hooks and catchy riffs, and indeed some of neue deutsche Welle's biggest, and most politically charged, hits came out of Berlin. Given Berlin's unique political situation, divided in two by the Berlin Wall, as well as the fact that it was a younger city, the angst of its youth was not postindustrial but post-nuclear.

Berlin's music scene had a reputation for being political and nihilistic. Groups from both East and West Berlin questioned German musical tradition and endorsed political protest on local, national, and international levels.[11] One *New Music Express (NME)* article described Berlin as "the final frontier: the city of dreams where all good suffering artists go to die." The city was seen as a "last outpost of the West" replete with a "mixture of squatters, stragglers and petty criminals tainting the state's vision of consumerism gone haywire," and most importantly, "The Wall, which . . . holds a violent fascination," casts a shadow over all of it.[12] But, life in the city at the end of the world was not without its charms. In a 1983 interview with *NME*, Blixa Bargeld, who was the front man of Einstürzende Neubauten, remarked, "It would be really hard to break down the wall . . . not so much because of the DDR but because without it there would be nothing really interesting anymore.

---

[11] Elizabeth Janick, *Recomposing German Music: Politics and Musical Tradition in Cold War Berlin* (Leiden: Brill, 2005), 275.
[12] Dele Fadele, "Einstürzende Neubauten: A Berlin of the Mind," *New Musical Express*, September 19, 1987.

It would be like living in West Germany and West Germany is totally uninteresting." The interviewer then quips, "In other words, thank you East Germany for the wall space upon which Einstürzende Neubauten write such arresting graffiti."[13] The high-tension political environment fueled the city's artistic output.

The ultimate irony is that out of the city most wedded to the "no future" mentality came the most hopeful event of the late twentieth century. The music journalist David Stubbs notes that, paradoxically, the Berlin scene "thrive[d] on a fascination with its own decay and its tragic geopolitical bisection," while "in reality it was laying the groundwork for the reunification of the city."[14] The nihilism of the Berlin scene had in fact worked to bring the two halves of the city together in a shared antistate, antiestablishment mentality, priming young people who had never known a unified Germany to jump at the opportunity to be one with each other.

Something that united many avant-garde bands, across local scenes, was the prevalence of women. Groups like Camilla Motor, Cosa Rosa, FEE, Jawoll, Lusthansa, Mona Mur & Die Mieter, Monopol, Nuala, Schlösser rechts, Seen links, Ski und der Rest, Vera Kaa, ZaZa, and ZeitGeist had female vocalists. However, an article in the May 1980 issue of *Sounds* about the state of women in rock and new wave music highlighted the potential superficiality of the female singer, pointing out that often "playing instruments was the man's thing,

[13]Chris Bohn, "Einstürzende Neubauten: Let's Hear It for the Untergang Show," *New Musical Express*, February 5, 1983.
[14]David Stubbs, *Future Days: Krautrock and the Building of Modern Germany* (London: Faber and Faber, 2014), 418.

women contributed—on rare occasions—a pretty picture as the singer."[15] Grauzone, Hans-A-Plast, and die Mimmi's were mixed-gender groups with multiple female members, and Carambolage, Firlefanz, Malaria!, Neonbabies, UnterRock, and Xmal Deutschland were composed entirely of women. Just because a band has one, or even all, female member(s) does not make it avant-garde or groundbreaking. Indeed, many commercial neue deutsche Welle acts, such as Innerdeutsche Beziehungen and Instant Music, had female vocalists, and it was not uncommon for avant-garde bands to incorporate faceless female vocals without substantively discussing gender in their music. In this manner, Haddon argues, "women in post-punk might be interpreted as a form of cultural capital, a marker of socially liberal distinction."[16] At the same time, many NDW artists continued to write sexist and objectifying songs. Even worse, they often obfuscated their sexist messages under the guise of irony. For example, when performing his band Hubert Kah's 1983 hit song "Einmal nur mit Erika" ("Just One Time with Erika"), singer Hubert Kemmler would don a pink straightjacket and be caressed by his bandmates with flowers, adopting a pseudo-feminine role (perhaps that of the titular Erika).

Many female NDW musicians wrote songs about their experiences as women in Germany, in context of both the musical scene and broader society. The frustration of West German women with their elected representatives (very few of whom were women) was understandable. The

---

[15] Jill Vaudeville, "Zwei und zwei sind nicht mehr vier—alle Mauern stürzen ein," *Sounds*, May 1980, 24–8.
[16] Haddon, *What Is Post-Punk?*, 131.

Christian Democratic Union, which governed Germany for most of the 1980s, is a center-right political party that values an understanding of life and human rights based on Christianity, an understanding that carries with it an inherent social conservatism. Like American women, after the Second World War, West German women were expected to return to the household. They could not work without their husband's permission until 1977 and their access to education was limited. Abortion is still a crime in Germany (though, before 12 weeks of pregnancy, it has not been punishable since 1976), and marital rape was completely legal until 1997. In Switzerland, the home of Liliput and Grauzone, women only attained the right to vote on a federal level in 1971. Though most Swiss cantons extended that right soon after, in the early 1970s, the canton of Appenzell Ausserrhoden did not implement full suffrage until 1990. That means that during the height of neue deutsche Welle, there were women in Switzerland who did not have the right to vote.

Gender relations in the postwar German-speaking world became a theme of many NDW songs. On the 1982 song "Muskeln" by Bärchen und die Milchbubis, lead singer Annette Grotkasten cheerfully sings about getting big and strong to attract romantic partners. The upbeat tone of the song pervades, even as Grotkasten begins to describe using her muscles to beat her romantic partner. "Muskeln" is a darkly ironic commentary on domestic violence and a discomfiting role reversal. The music video also plays with gender roles, showing Grotkasten in a muscle shirt, with a short haircut, flexing in a boxing ring, surrounded by her bandmates and nearly naked bodybuilders. While singing a line about how "stepping" (interpreted both as an exercise step and kicking as physical violence) keeps one young and healthy, Grotkasten mimes the movement in dance, drawing attention to the malapropos heels she wears. This costuming works both as visual humor and as a reminder to the viewer that Grotkasten is only playing the role of aggressor and, in reality, is more likely to have been a victim of gendered violence than a perpetrator.

Bärchen und die Milchbubis are also uniquely innovative for their song "Tagebuch" ("Diary") the rare neue deutsche Welle song to discuss a lesbian relationship. Overall, homosexuality is far less discussed in neue deutsche Welle than gender, save one very notable exception: Deutsch Amerikanische Freundschaft. Known for their sweaty, rhythmic club music, the duo of Robert Görl and Gabi Delgado-López became icons on the international gay scene, more for their image—pulsing synth beats and leather outfits—than their actual identities (Görl was straight and Delgado-López bisexual). Even aesthetic provocations such as these were meaningful in West Germany. Sex between men had only been decriminalized in 1969 and then only for those older than twenty-one. The law that had banned it, called Paragraph 175, had existed since 1871, but it was made significantly more stringent (requiring less physical evidence of intercourse and carrying a higher penalty) in 1935 under the Nazi regime—it was this version of the law that the FRG kept on the books until 1969, and a form of Paragraph 175 remained until 1994 when the age of consent was equalized for hetero- and homosexual couples. Furthermore, the church still held powerful sway in society. In this climate, even more mild insinuations of non-heteronormative sexuality were radical.

NDW artists also took an irreverent approach to gender. For instance, die Mimmi's, a Bremen-based group with several female members, 1982 single "Wir Stehen Auf SV Werder" ("We Love [Football Club] SV Werder") was a semi-ironic send-up of German football culture, not unlike New Order's 1990 single, "World in Motion." The A-side, "Deutscher Meister Wird Der SVW" ("SVW Will be the German Champion") ostensibly cheers on local football team SV Werder, which had at the time just reentered the first-rank German Bundesliga and would go on to have several years of competitive success. The song's accompanying music video, simplistic lyrics, and jolly tone poke fun at the concept of a football anthem. Shots of the band, dressed like bookish punks, festooned with scarves and hats in SVW colors, awkwardly dancing and playing their instruments on a snow-covered football pitch, the stadium empty of fans, paint a humorous contrast to typical images of macho German football culture. Even bands without any female members made songs with feminist messages.[17]

Disappointingly, plenty of sexist narratives persist in the neue deutsche Welle canon. There are many examples of songs that objectify and degrade women or tell childish narratives of men desperate for sex. The most notable, but also complex, case surrounds the Jeanny series, a group of several songs, some more official than others (many were released as posthumous cash-grabs), by the Austrian artist Falco. The first, and most important, part of the series, "Jeanny," released in 1985, has ambiguous lyrics that describe a woman in distress, from the point of view of a man who is obsessed with her—possibly her forbidden love, but also perhaps a stalker, rapist, or

---

[17] For example, the band Clit's 1982 song "Frau sein" ("Being a Woman"), which was critical of beauty standards.

even murderer. The music video, which depicts a kidnapping, seems to endorse the darker readings. The lead female role is played by the fifteen-year-old Theresa Guggenberger, who tries to escape Falco in several instances. The song was seen by feminist groups as glorifying violence against women and was boycotted and removed from broadcast by several German radio and television stations. The song's follow-up, "Coming Home (Jeanny Part 2, ein Jahr danach)," released one year later, represents something of a redemption arc for Falco's character and was an attempt to recast the song by the artist. The insanity of the protagonist is foregrounded, even as his desire to change and redeem himself is articulated. Guggenberger returned for the music video, but this time is styled and shot as a more active, powerful figure. Still, the fact that this kind of narrative became so popular, and in turn provoked such a strong reaction, reveals that even as women in NDW used both politicized and ironic language to criticize misogynistic society, men traded on violence against women to serve a narrative function.

Another prominent trend in avant-garde neue deutsche Welle music was the importance of performance art. While live performance has always been crucial to the formation of musical communities, even more so under-resourced ones, such as punks and their aesthetic descendants, performance art is slightly different. Neue deutsche Welle artists like die Tödliche Doris and Minus Delta T used performance art in order to highlight their political messages and access an avant-garde register of aesthetic communication.

NDW performance art worked in two modes. The first was a kind of anti-music—practically unlistenable noise. The prototypical example of this type of "music" is Einstürzende Neubauten, whose early recordings lack both rhythm and melody, resembling industrial field recordings more than any kind of recognizable music. It is necessary to mention here an even earlier ancestor of performance art in neue deutsche Welle: the band Kraftwerk. Founded in 1970 in Düsseldorf, Kraftwerk preceded the NDW scene by nearly a decade. The band is also recognized today as a pioneer of electronic music, that would go on to influence not only German artists but also international groups such as New Order and Depeche Mode. It is worthwhile to consider how Kraftwerk's music was viewed at the time and the effect it would come to have on neue deutsche Welle, in order to better understand the relationship between performance art and music.

Kraftwerk not only made use of the most cutting-edge new synthesizers and drum machines; they also experimented with technology and pushed the borders of what was considered musical production by invoking the computer as a fully-fledged band member, manipulating recordings using tape overlays, and bringing the electrical functioning of modern musical instruments to the fore (e.g., by using the metal contacts in knitting needles to play). In addition, they cultivated an aesthetically minded image, all wearing matching suits and styling their hair in a neat, business-like fashion. At the time, one would not have been remiss to call Kraftwerk a collective of new media artists. Because their innovations were picked up by musicians and brought into the avant-garde scene, and then the mainstream, they are thought of today as a band. This example serves to show how complex categorization is and how it can be manipulated to tell various historical narratives.

NDW performance also consisted of art projects and the involvement of bands in activities that were distinctly nonmusical. The best example of this kind of performance art is the Austrian group Minus Delta T, who would stage, according to Kurt Dahlke, "really tough performances. Dangerous performances," in which the audience was prevented from leaving the venue even as the band "poured water into the room. . . . Then they threw plaster in huge amounts so you were standing in white mud. And altogether with very loud electronic music. And then they would throw dead fishes, everything started to stink and the people went very aggressive and wanted to go out. But there was no way out."[18] Minus Delta T's most extensive performance art project involved a giant stone, which they attempted to transport all the way from England to China. The goal was to have the stone make a kind of religious pilgrimage, visiting sacred sites all around the world, while the band brought along a recorder and made an album out of their travels. The entire project was financed through art world connections.[19] The neue deutsche Welle scene and the German modern art scene were intertwined. At one point, Dahlke worked with a contemporary artist friend in order to get his record company, Ata Tak, out of debt, and the German artist Martin Kippenberger managed the Berlin NDW club SO36 from 1978.[20]

---

[18] Hanna Bächer, "The Experimental Life of Pyrolator," *Red Bull Music Academy*, April 26, 2019, https://daily.redbullmusicacademy.com/2019/04/pyrolator -interview.
[19] Ibid.
[20] Ibid.; Ji-Hun Kim, "The Relationship Between Berlin Club Culture and Contemporary Art," *Red Bull Music Academy*, https://daily.redbullmusicacademy .com/2018/08/berlin-club-culture-and-art.

Political messaging is not enough to distinguish performance art from musical performance—Minus Delta T's rock pilgrimage, for example, is just as politically nonsensical and culturally confused as many pop recordings that use Japanese imagery as orientalist set-dressing. Intent and influence patterns may be the most important factor, both in the classification of music as performance art and for assigning categories of avant-garde versus commercial in neue deutsche Welle music, a distinction that this book will continue to investigate. First, it is necessary to return to a crucial piece of historical context.

3 In the Shadow of the Wall

The Berlin scene was not only a center of neue deutsche Welle music but also a Cold War pop-cultural touchstone. The image of a divided, heavily militarized Berlin centers on the Berlin Wall, an almost 100-mile-long, 10-feet-tall concrete barrier with watchtowers. Adjacent to the wall lay a "death strip" of open land in which East German citizens attempting to flee to the West were shot. Construction of the wall began overnight in 1961 with the erection of barbed wire, which was fortified as time went on. After their victory in the Second World War, the allied governments (the United States, Great Britain, the Soviet Union, and at the last minute, France) divided not only the territory of greater Germany but also the city of Berlin (which sat in the east of the country) into four (and then later two, as the United States, the United Kingdom, and France combined their administration) zones. The wall ran along this boundary.

Until 1961, travel between East and West Berlin had not been highly restricted. Many East Berliners worked in the West and traveled daily between the two halves of the city. As economic disparity between East and West Germany grew, more and more East Germans began to take advantage of the Berlin loophole to leave the socialist country. This created a massive brain drain; the population loss was unsustainable for the German Democratic Republic. The exact functioning of the wall was not formalized until 1971, under the Quadripartite Agreement, which formalized the division of the city that had begun ten years earlier with the construction of the wall.[1]

Despite the divided nature of the city, the scenes of East and West Berlin were not drastically different, and cultural communication across the wall was very possible. The GDR was more restrictive, but by the 1980s, the government was allowing more Western musicians to perform inside its borders and releasing their music on the state-run VEB pop label, Amiga. Domestic musicians, even those who were part of the official aboveground cultural system, such as the band Pankow, no longer couched their critiques of the state in metaphor.[2] Youths from the East could also meet with the West by eavesdropping on stadium performances taking place in the other half of Berlin. This phenomenon was known to concert organizers, who sometimes turned up and pointed their speakers for the benefit of East Germans, and by police, who often violently broke up the gathered crowds.[3]

Many NDW musicians turned their attention to the city. Einstürzende Neubauten's 1981 song "Steh auf Berlin" ("I Love Berlin") opens with the noise of a jackhammer, before transitioning into a repetitive chant. The lead singer Blixa

---

[1]"Quadripartite Agreement of September 3, 1971," in *The Berlin Settlement: The Quadripartite Agreement on Berlin and the Supplementary Arrangements* (Wiesbaden: Press and Information Office of the Government of the Federal Republic of Germany, 1972), 7–9.
[2]David Robb, "Censorship, Dissent and the Metaphorical Language of GDR Rock," in *Popular Music in Eastern Europe: Breaking the Cold War Paradigm*, ed. Ewa Mazierska (London: Palgrave Macmillan, 2006), 109–28.
[3]Janick, *Recomposing German Music*, 296–7.

Bargeld proclaims his love for "decay," "sickness," and "decline," and declares that he stands at the end times, playing into the nihilism of the Berlin scene.

This embrace of decrepitude can be seen in a more sophisticated form in the 1980 Ideal song "Berlin," which chronicles a day out on the town. Despite the presence of fare-checkers (an agent of the state who made sure that German transit riders paid the cost of ridership with random checks) on the train, the bleak, gray city buildings, the presence of junkies on the street, and the ever-present wall, the singer's happy mood does not waver. She reaffirms her love of Berlin and is able to make it to the dance floor by the end of the night. She is also unabashedly metropolitan, delighting in the Turkish melodies she hears passing through the city and eating pizza out of her hand like an American. Here there is also the rejection of staunch Germanness in favor of the cultures of Turkish immigrants and American globalizers, exemplifying the forward-thinking youth culture of Berlin.

The physical venues of Berlin where this music was performed were also important. The club provided a space in which NDW and its antecedent, dance music, could develop real communities. By the 1980s, even East Germany had developed its own nightlife scene, which saw the appearance of public clubs and bars.[4] One journalist wrote that in East Berlin, "Queues . . . are at the entrances of restaurants and nightclubs instead of outside food shops as in Poland." Oftentimes to get in, you would have to pay a bribe or

---

[4] Jens Richard Giersdorf, *The Body of the People: East German Dance since 1945* (Madison: University of Wisconsin Press, 2013), 124.

leverage social connections.[5] This shows that going out was a popular experience that people were willing to sacrifice for and indicates the importance of interpersonal networks.

Clubs were also an important venue for gays and lesbians to socialize and express themselves more freely. In this respect, East Germany was more liberal than its Western counterpart. In 1968, the socialist country decriminalized gay sex, effectively becoming not only the most progressive country in the Soviet bloc but also more progressive than even West Germany.[6] The GDR even organized "social nights for gays in the state-controlled youth clubs," though this was in part a ploy to draw them away from activist groups organized by churches.[7] Outside of the officially sanctioned clubs, gay venues like Ellis Bierbar continued to draw partygoers from West Berlin even after the Berlin Wall was erected. Such clubs were not illegal, but police would still find excuses to raid them.[8] The gay club became something of a gray zone: not expressly illegal but a target of law enforcement. This made clubbing while gay a political act, and the clubs themselves became centers of community formation and organization.

Neue deutsche Welle also existed in East Germany. Initially, NDW was seen by the German Democratic Republic as a positive but foreign cultural force. GDR cultural administrators saw the same antiestablishment, left-leaning expressions of

---

[5] Emmanuel Fessy, "In East Berlin, Saturday Night Fever Is Over Food, Not Disco," *The Hartford Courant*, September 3, 1981, D12.
[6] Giersdorf, *The Body of the People*, 124.
[7] Denis M. Sweet, "A Literature of 'Truth': Writing by Gay Men in East Germany," *Studies in 20th Century Literature* 22, iss. 1 (1998), 207.
[8] Jennifer V. Evans, *Life among the Ruins: Cityscape and Sexuality in Cold War Berlin* (England: Palgrave Macmillan, 2011), 179.

youth discontent with West German society that this book has delineated. For the East German government, anything that disrupted West German society or called into question the supremacy of its capitalist, Western-oriented way of life was a boon. This policy often went far further than simple support for a socially critical genre of pop music; the East German intelligence service would indeed support both left-wing domestic terror groups like the Rote Armee Fraktion and right-wing neo-Nazis in West Germany. It was a comparatively simple matter for them to endorse neue deutsche Welle as an artistic movement, which they did. For example, the *Jugendlexikon*, a pop-cultural youth encyclopedia published by a state-owned firm, correctly identifies the roots of NDW in English punk, emphasizing the shared struggle to record in expensive, private studios and problems of youth unemployment and alienation, which were common across the UK and the FRG. The *Jugendlexikon* criticizes neue deutsche Welle for only "actualizing, but not analyzing" these problems and not being able to solve them. Another problem identified by the *Jugendlexikon* is the rapid commodification of the genre by American-owned record labels, such as WEA and CBS, who neutered any possibility of capitalist critique in favor of mass-producing dance-friendly hits.[9] The East German party line reproduces the narrative of the "two sides" of neue deutsche Welle. It also implies that it would be impossible for a genre like NDW to exist in the East because of the educational

[9] Hella Brock and Kleinschmidt, Christoph (eds.), *Jugendlexikon: Musik* (Leipzig, Deutsche Demokratische Republik: VEB Bibliographisches Institut, 1983), 248–9.

opportunities, job security, and classless society that citizens of the GDR supposedly enjoyed.

To an extent, that sentiment was correct, insofar as neue deutsche Welle was critical of consumer society. While East German patterns of consumption were some of the most Western-like of the socialist bloc (far more than in the Soviet Union proper, for example), they were not comparable to those of the new middle class in West Germany. Other experiences, such as living under an unchangeable government ruled by a few, staid interest groups or the complete domination of the press by a few industry figures, were universal to both East and West Germans. The only difference was that in West Germany, these forces were controlled by private industry and in the East, they were controlled by the Communist Party.

Similar antiestablishment sentiments appeared in underground East German music of the 1980s. Bands like Parole Emil, Schleim-Keim, and Zwitschermaschine expressed frustration with the stagnation of life under socialism; the East German government responded with aggression and surveillance. It would be a stretch to call this scene new wave or even post-punk—these were punk bands.[10] Aside from the subject matter they discussed, there were technical limitations that prevented the East German punk scene from becoming post-punk or new wave. They operated in an underground

---

[10] Two contemporary documentaries about punks (as well as other fringe subcultures) in East Germany, produced by the state-run film studio DEFA (Deutsche Film AG), are Günter Jordan, *Einmal in der Woche schrein* (German Democratic Republic: DEFA-Studio für Dokumentarfilme, 1982), and Roland Steiner, *Unsere Kinder* (German Democratic Republic: DEFA-Studio für Dokumentarfilme, 1989). The former was filmed in 1982 but not approved for official release until 1989.

manner. They were not DIY by choice but out of necessity. It was hard for them to acquire instruments, find venues to play in, and especially to produce recorded music—most surviving recordings are bootleg cassette tapes of live performances. The state had a monopoly on the kind of synth instruments and high-tech production equipment (to the extent that it was even accessible in the East, as it was often imported) needed to produce the new wave sound.

One East German neue deutsche Welle star, in a sense, is Nina Hagen. Both as a solo artist and as a part of the Nina Hagen Band (whose other members later went on to perform as Spliff), Hagen had several important NDW hits. She was born in East Germany and recorded a few singles there as a state-produced pop artist. When her stepfather, the East German songwriter Wolf Biermann, was forcibly exiled while on a state-sanctioned tour of West Germany, Hagen followed him there and signed with CBS Records. It was only in West Germany that she came to make music in the mold of the NDW sound. Her stardom, if not her music, was inflected by her experience growing up in East Germany; it gave Hagen a rebellious edge. Upon the release of her debut Western album *Nina Hagen Band*, in 1978, *Sounds* declared "She came, sang and conquered," a politically tinged reference with a Caesarian inflection that nods to both Hagen's arrival in the Federal Republic of Germany and the domination of her new album over the magazine's various national popularity polls.[11]

However, neue deutsche Welle is not a strictly West German, capitalist genre. NDW music was being made in

---

[11]"Ergebnisse National," *Sounds*, March 1979, 9.

East Germany—just not underground. The government itself produced the music. Responding to the demand by the East German public for synth sounds and modern dance tracks, cultural officials, working through Amiga, began to produce their own neue deutsche Welle groups, such as Brigitte Stefan and Meridian, Juckreiz, Petra Zieger and Smokings, and Prinzz. These groups largely played in a pop-rock-style derivative of West German, British, and American new wave hits. The themes of the songs were banal, discussing relationships or, occasionally, kitsch elements of East German life like Freikörperkultur ("free body culture," colloquially known as "FKK" or "naturism" in English, the practice of spending time outdoors in the nude). These groups often made use of visual tropes seen in West German NDW, such as big, bleached hair, colorful clothing, and a female singer supported by an all-male backing band. In this sense, the neue deutsche Welle that was produced in East Germany was commercial, even as it was made by the socialist government.

The musical scenes of both West and East Germany were simultaneously more united and more divided than is commonly assumed. Both Germanys produced commercial, formulaic NDW, and they both had alternative scenes. Their independent scenes were in communication with one another, and the mainstream cultural apparatus of the German Democratic Republic took inspiration from its counterpart in the Federal Republic of Germany. It remains important to emphasize that in East Germany, the independent scene was forced underground by government oppression, whereas in the West, its countercultural traits were more thematic.

The Space Race

While the political realities of the Cold War affected the manner in which neue deutsche Welle music was produced on both sides of the Iron Curtain, the broader cultural context of the war also inspired NDW artists. Since the latter half of the twentieth century, space has captivated the imagination of people around the globe. West Germans were particularly keen to the imagery and technologies critical to the Cold War. Their country was a hot spot in the Cold War, the place where the United States and Soviet Union came nose-to-nose. The German pop cultural fascination with space peaked in the 1980s when the domestic music scene boomed in accordance with the rise of neue deutsche Welle. NDW artists discuss space from diverse viewpoints. They appeal to world powers to keep space a peaceful realm and protest when the Cold War makes incursions upon the stars. They also idealize space, engaging in the deification of astronauts.

The main characterization of space in German NDW music was positive. Both postwar, antinationalist pacifism and the Western panic that followed the 1957 launch of Sputnik, the first man-made satellite, by the Soviets, faded rapidly from the German imagination. In his detailed analysis of German media, the historian and ARTE program director Bernd Mütter writes that while military concerns featured significantly in West German media for the first nine months following the launch, the share of media attention given to these concerns quickly fell off. By August 1958, military conceptualizations of outer space had fallen from a 26.2 percent plurality down to 7.1 percent, ahead only of peacekeeping, whereas scientific and technological perceptions grew from an already large 22.3 percent up to 26 percent, more than double the share of any other category.[12] The conflict in the German perception of spaceflight was not whether it was a warlike or pacifist pursuit, but rather, as Mütter presents it, between universalist and nationalist framings. He asserts that Germans could choose to see their country as a participant in a broader, global effort to reach the stars or instead glorify its own unique technological advancements. The former interpretation allowed Germans to ride in the slipstream of other nations, while the latter emphasized Germany's superiority over less advanced countries.[13] This conflict is mirrored in German participation in international space programs, like the European Space Research Organization (ESRO) and the European Launcher Development Organization (ELDO), in the 1960s. German officials contributed heavily to these early international projects out of a desire to rebuild their technological capacity in a palatable manner.[14] By the time Germany took part in the founding of the European Space Agency (ESA) in 1975, its national capability had been restored, and it was ready to commit to a leadership role in a more integrated organization.

Neue deutsche Welle music likewise reflects this complicated, but generally positive, relationship with space.

[12] Bernd Mütter, "*Per Media Ad Astra?* Outer Space in West Germany's Media, 1957-87," in *Imagining Outer Space: European Astroculture in the Twentieth Century*, ed. Alexander C. T. Geppert (London: Palgrave Macmillan, 2012), 169.
[13] Ibid., 172.
[14] Kevin Madders, *A New Force at a New Frontier: Europe's Development in the Space Field in the Light of Its Main Actors, Policies, Law, and Activities from Its Beginnings Up to the Present* (Cambridge: Cambridge University Press, 1997), 83–7.

For example, the 1984 song "Der lustige Astronaut" ("The Cheerful Astronaut"), by die Ärzte, takes a lyrically dark song and makes it comical. The band's titular astronaut thinks of leaving behind Earth, the only home he has ever known, with nonchalant glee. His dismal lyrics contrast with a swinging, happy rhythm. In fact, "Der lustige Astronaut" almost sounds like a children's song. This dramatic juxtaposition serves to further the deification of the astronaut figure. Though the song could be read as an ironic criticism of risky space travel programs, the lyrics never become specific or self-aware enough to suggest more serious objections. Indeed, such duality in music does invite accusations of inauthenticity. The historian Cyrus Shahan, for example, accuses die Ärzte of being a "fun punk" band, "trafficking in punk aesthetic performances and angst (social demise)," but ultimately being "too choreographed and inauthentic."[15] Shahan is in a certain way correct. Die Ärzte never broach significant social criticism and, in this respect, they exemplify NDW bands that used the aesthetics of the underground to make banal music.

A more nuanced and popular tale of a drifting astronaut is Peter Schilling's 1982 German-language cover of David Bowie's "Space Oddity," titled "Major Tom (Völlig Losgelöst)" ("Major Tom (Completely Cut Off)"). The song is a darker, yet no less heroic, take on space travel. In Schilling's version, it can be argued that the titular astronaut, Major Tom, perishes, but in his last moments achieves some kind of spiritual enlightenment.

---

[15] Cyrus Shahan, "Fehlfarben and German Punk: The Making of 'No Future,'" in *German Pop Music: A Compilation*, ed. Schütte (Berlin: Walter de Gruyter GmbH, 2017), 129, 112.

In the final verses of the song, Schilling describes an unclear fate for Tom. Just as people begin to mourn him, he says he is returning home, only to begin to grow cold and continue to drift in space. His "return" is not so literal. In helpless isolation, he finds a guiding light and is freed of all worries and stress. Because of Tom's implied death, "Major Tom (Völlig Losgelöst)" is often interpreted by journalists as being a "troubling tale of an astronaut adrift in outer space;" however, Schilling himself was always more concerned with the dangers posed by the military applications of orbital technology to society than spaceflight and the personal endangerment of astronauts. He is quoted as saying, "No one is happy about the [American Pershing II] missiles coming to our country . . . It's a crazy situation when I can . . . see the missiles out my window."[16] Schilling is referring to the installation of American armaments in West Germany in the early 1980s, which went forward despite protests. In his cover, Schilling makes no explicit allusions to military applications of technology; just because he was opposed to the military application of space technology does not mean he was troubled by all its potential uses. If anything, the song is vague and can just as easily be interpreted as hippie-like and feeble. One opinionated journalist, lamenting the days when "the universe was like the western prairie, terrain with lots of room for the expansion of manly virtues," contrasts Bowie's heroic Major Tom with what he perceives as a "musical atmosphere reminiscent of getting lightly drunk on beer on

---

[16]Patrick Goldstein, "Pop Eye: In Germany, It's Agitrock," *Los Angeles Times*, October 30, 1983, U84.

a balmy summer evening" in Schilling's version.[17] Schilling's Major Tom lackadaisically embraces his demise, welcomes it even. The cover idealizes a lonely death in space by portraying it as an opportunity for making peace with oneself and finding enlightenment in mortality.

A particularly revealing subgenre of neue deutsche Welle space songs are those that feature alien characters. By the 1980s, aliens were commonly seen in science fiction media; these German extraterrestrials are unique in their uniform goodness. While they may be wise or mischievous, noble or thrill-seeking, all of them mean no harm and are a positive force. Rhetorically, aliens often function as devices by which Germans can self-examine their own national character.

For example, Andreas Dorau's 1981 song "Fred vom Jupiter" ("Fred from Jupiter") is about a handsome alien who crash-lands on Earth and is received with goodwill, especially by the women of Earth. Soon all the human men become jealous and Fred, not comprehending their evil reaction, decides it is best for him to leave, though the women plead with him to stay. Fred is the tragic hero of the song. He is too good for Earth but rather than attempting to stay and impose his will, he leaves of his own volition, to prevent further conflicts. Though he is the titular character, the song is in many ways not about Fred. By adopting the perspective of an alien, "Fred vom Jupiter" depicts humans as the foreign quantity, enabling them to be more easily criticized. In an inversion of the trope, it is not a brave, human astronaut who conquers the frontier of space and discovers "savage" aliens. Rather, a peaceful, idealized

---

[17]"Popmusik: So gräßlich häßlich," *Der Spiegel*, v. 35, August 29, 1983.

alien leaves humanity lest he plunge the planet into an all-out battle of the sexes. Dorau's depiction of Fred is in line with the thinking of German science fiction author Kurd Laßwitz (1848–1910), an early pioneer of the genre, whose alien characters functioned "as projections of possible future developments of life" and "the potential of ethical progress."[18] Not only is Fred the ideal physical specimen, his morality is beyond the pale and he is self-sacrificing.

Planet Earth is also a grim place, deprived of love and ruled by hate, in "Codo," a 1983 song by the band Deutsch-Österreichisches Feingefühl (DÖF). That is, until the titular spaceship Codo arrives. Despite plots by the earthbound authorities to kill Codo by shooting down the spaceship, Codo triumphs and brings love to Earth. Once again, the alien plays the role of a benevolent, wise outsider, who comes to bring love and happiness to Earth. In "Codo," the humans get a happy ending, as the global hate regime is overthrown. We are the savages, and Codo is the conquering hero, who uses love and not guns. It is no wonder that the same journalist who derided Schilling also called "Codo" "infantile," "unintentional comedy," and proclaimed, first "Hippie culture hyped-up space with psychedelic fantasies, and then the new children's films by Lucas and Spielberg [*Star Wars*] banished the grown man from the expanse of the universe."[19] "Codo" was a hit the summer this article was written, but the journalist dismisses it as a song without the substance or gravitas of previous science fiction. Nonetheless, it is this

---

[18]Thomas Brandstetter, "Imagining Inorganic Life: Crystalline Aliens in Science and Fiction," in *Imagining Outer Space: European Astroculture in the Twentieth Century*, ed. Alexander C. T. Geppert (London: Palgrave Macmillan, 2012), 73.
[19]"Popmusik: So gräßlich häßlich."

abstraction from real life that allows "Codo" to function as an agent of social critique. The media historian Stevphen Shukaitis argues that "outer space . . . creates a space for engagement with weighty issues . . . while allowing an enticing playfulness to be employed."[20] This is exactly what is happening in "Codo." Playful voice effect technology and a hyperbolically pacifist alien character obfuscate the song's deeper commentary on hatefulness and division in global society.

Postwar politics also played a large part in shaping the German public's view of spaceflight as a Cold War technology. While spaceflight technology does have some purely scientific applications, it is undeniable that many of the field's most ambitious projects would not have been supported if they did not also have military applications. A particular soft spot for Germans was the use of rockets to launch nuclear-armed missiles. Divided Germany epitomized a Cold War flashpoint. Germans saw themselves as vulnerable residents of a valuable borderland, the first to go if the US and USSR ever made good on their rhetoric. Accordingly, West German politicians thought it vital that they balance their alliance with America with outreach to its Eastern counterpart. When the United States asked for involvement in the Strategic Defense Initiative (SDI), a Reagan-era missile defense system program dubbed "Star Wars" in common parlance, it created a great deal of controversy, which turned to outright animosity after the project fell apart due to lack of technological ability and

In the Shadow of the Wall

[20] Stevphen Shukaitis, "Space Is the (Non)place: Martians, Marxists, and the Outer Space of the Radical Imagination," in *Space Travel and Culture: From Apollo to Space Tourism*, ed. David Bell and Martin Parker (Malden, MA: Wiley-Blackwell, 2009), 99.

political goodwill. More expressly scientific programs like Spacelab, a laboratory module for the Space Shuttle jointly developed by NASA and the European Space Agency (ESA, of which West Germany was a founding member), were seen as opportunities both to grow domestic industry and for Germany to demonstrate its loyalty to the United States, even in the midst of *Ostpolitik*.[21] A throughline can be seen in German consciousness: a desire to keep space free from the Cold War conflicts threatening to consume Earth.

In his 1986 song "Cowboyz and Indianz," the Austrian singer Falco considers the fickle nature of success in the Space Race and how it throws all adjacent countries into tumult too. In the song, Falco describes the actions of the two world superpowers as no more considered than the whims of children. Their feelings change day to day. Because the Americans are undertaking a space project, so too must the Soviets. At the end of the day, both powers are sitting in the same pub, while countries like Germany are stuck in the middle, carrying out the superpowers' glorified astro-military projects, like the SDI. The SDI would become a much-maligned failure, but at the time of the song's release the question of German participation divided the country. Generally, the ruling, right-wing Christian Democratic Union supported the plan, which aimed to create a defensive missile network capable of shooting down nuclear attacks, as a means of solidifying West Germany's alliance with the United States, while the oppositional Social Democratic Party did not support the SDI, believing it would create a new

---

[21] John Krige, *NASA in the World: Fifty Years of International Collaboration in Space* (New York: Palgrave Macmillan, 2013), 120–1.

arms race, further hastening mutually assured destruction. No strict battle lines were drawn and German society was overall very conflicted.[22] Falco's song, then, exemplifies the pacifist view. While the music historian Ewa Mazierska interprets the whole of the *Emotional* album, from which the song comes, as a "tribute to American popular culture," it is hard to see "Cowboyz and Indianz" as even tongue-in-cheek praise.[23] At the end of the song, Falco adopts the persona of a child, pleading for his father as an unnamed aggressor opens fire. The assessment of one music journalist, who saw Falco as "a man [who had once been] so keen to crack America that he let other bands cover his potential hit ('Der Kommissar'), but now, with America at his feet, [he] is openly anti-American," seems more accurate.[24] It would appear that there was indeed a limit to postwar German gratitude toward their American allies and, as the United States became increasingly entangled in global conflict, Germans became more outspokenly anti-American. These sentiments then manifested as opposition to joint space projects, especially when these projects had military purposes.

Even scientific projects could be maligned. The band Fehlfarben's song "Ein Jahr (es geht voran)" ("One Year (It Goes On)") asserts that even as the world is going to hell, time goes on and the people in charge are unperturbed, all while historical amnesia spreads among the masses. Fehlfarben criticizes not

---

[22] Klaus Gottstein, "The Debate on the SDI in the Federal Republic of Germany," in *Strategic Defenses and the Future of the Arms Race: A Pugwash Symposium*, ed. John Holdren and Joseph Rotblat (London: Macmillan, 1987), 151–61.

[23] Ewa Mazierska, *Falco and Beyond: Neo Nothing Post of All* (Sheffield: Equinox, 2013), 99.

[24] Simon Witter, "Brahms, Liszt and . . . Falco?" *New Music Express*, 1986.

just joint military projects but also scientific ones. As the band saw it, any partnership with the Americans'"gray B-movie hero" president, Ronald Reagan (a common target of ire, he was rated the number one "Public Figure on the Outs" of 1981 by *Sounds* readers[25]), represented acquiescence to the United States' ignorant worldview. Jäger writes that an ironic commentary on "the notion of progress" is "conjured up at the end of each line" through the repetition of the parenthetical refrain, which stands in sharp contrast to the "catastrophes," listed by the song just prior.[26] The American conception of success demands ever-increasing wealth, happiness, and power, even at the cost of relationships with allies. Indeed, Spacelab was seen, in retrospect, as something of an American betrayal of Germany and the European Space Agency. The European Space Agency was to build the first Spacelab module and then hand it over to the United States, which was contracted to use it to run one further mission. There was some hope that they might choose to continue the project, but NASA indeed stopped at their contractual obligation.[27] Fehlfarben saw Spacelab as just another in a long line of American failures that would lead to the annihilation of the US, USSR, and every innocent country in between. One article, in the music publication *Melody Maker*, opened with the following as a kind of summation of Fehlfarben's overarching message, "Under the nuclear shadow, something stirs. Looking West, it decides to reject the old men's fear and guilt. If the sands of time are turning radioactive, why

---

[25]"Poll '81," *Sounds*, February 1981, 11.
[26] Jäger, "Ripples on a Bath of Steel," 133.
[27] Krige, *NASA in the World*, 121.

not go down smiling and waving instead of huddling under the nuclear umbrella, pale and shaking with fear?"[28] "Ein Jahr (Es geht voran)" maintains this cheerier tone, conveying the dominant pacifist tendency of neue deutsche Welle music.

The most famous NDW song of all is also a peace anthem. Nena's 1983 worldwide hit "99 Luftballons" ("99 Balloons") tells the story of war ministers and generals mistaking balloons for enemy UFOs and, in their haste to shoot them down, starting World War III. Though the story line of "99 Luftballons" is clear, the song avoids referencing any specific state or politician. This is intentional. One music journalist notes that "the Nenas [sic] already shrug off the 'protest music' tag," and not unjustly, as "'99 Luftballons' is an anti-war song, but not politically so; it's much more of a love-ravaged-by-war pessimistic romance."[29] Such appeals for peace by West Germany's postwar generation were in part a reaction against the violent crimes of their parents and grandparents; it is no coincidence that these appeals frequently appear in space songs. Postwar German disarmament meant the country's cosmic ambitions could not be tied to military aims, unlike in the United States. West German space projects either aimed to build a brighter, technologically advanced future or celebrated the glory of their own scientific advances.[30] Space was not seen as the next domino to fall to communism; the Germans perceived it to be utopian, an ideological tabula rasa.

---

[28] Adam Sweeting, "Fehlfarben: Before the Deluge," *Melody Maker*, July 31, 1982.
[29] Richard Riegel, "Nena: 99 Luftballons (Epic)," *Creem*, June 1984.
[30] Mütter, "*Per Media Ad Astra?*," 166.

Other NDW songs about space were more explicit in their criticism of the United States and Soviet Union. The band FEE's song "Amerika" is sarcastically jingoistic, supposedly extolling the many achievements of the United States. At a frenetic pace, the singer lists off American "firsts," including positive accomplishments, like the Moon landing and rock'n'roll music, but also darkly satirical negatives, like the development of the atom bomb and the invasion of Vietnam, before pointing out, teasingly, that though the Americans were first to the Moon, the Soviets did beat them to Afghanistan. The juxtaposition of the Moon with Cold War battlegrounds (Vietnam, Afghanistan) is not coincidental. As noted in the discussion of peace songs, Germans recognized that the world powers, namely America, saw space as a military frontier, a militaristic attitude that put countries caught in the middle, like Germany, in danger. Literally a divided country, Germany would be the first battleground if the Cold War were to heat up. In this context, the launch of Sputnik in 1957 and the beginning of the "Space Race" was not a force for national unity (whether in celebration or oppositional mobilization) but an "immediate [military] threat."[31] Sputnik represented the danger of another home turf war, not just the technological advancement of the Soviet Union. Neue deutsche Welle artists did not see themselves as citizens of a warmongering nation; it was the US and USSR that the world had to be wary of.

Kosmonautentraum's 1982 song "Kosmonaut" combines the musical influences of the more gothic, machinated post-punk subgenre cold wave with a repetitive, chant-like lyrical

---

[31] Ibid., 168.

delivery to emphasize its nihilistic critique of the Soviet Union. The singer describes dancing as the world ends, equating the spinning, lonesome flight of the cosmonaut to a party at the end of the world. Just as the space traveler could at any moment experience any one of seemingly infinite disasters and be lost forever, so could West Germany and, by extension, the rest of the world. It is no coincidence that in NDW songs, America is seen as an aggressive, cunning enemy with soldiers on the ground in every country (and beyond). Conversely, the USSR is portrayed as barely having control over their astronaut. During this time, Soviet kitsch pervaded German pop music. It was used to give songs a funky, "exotic" twist. See Boney M.'s 1978 smash disco hit "Rasputin," which casts the Russian imperial mystic as the lead in a dance floor romp. Closer in terms of genre is Stricher's 1982 song "Ja padam u Kosmos" ("I'm Going to Space"), whose title is rendered in pseudo-Russian. Kosmonautentraum employed this same strategy to full effect. Their album was titled *Juri Gagarin* and featured a picture of said cosmonaut taken from the East German propaganda newspaper *Sowjetunion Heute* ("*Soviet Union Today*"), although some listeners thought it was the band's singer in costume.[32] Kosmonautentraum's music had serious artistic merit as well. The journalist and sociologist Christof Meueler characterizes it as "far out" and sounding like what "spiral nebulae" look like.[33] They were considered high concept despite their pop culture references. Due to

---

[32] Christof Mueuler, *Das ZickZack Prinzip: Alfred Hilsberg—Ein Leben für den Underground* (Munich: Wilhelm Heyne Verlag, 2016).
[33] Ibid.

some of the song's more darkly poetic, "spacey" elements, its kitsch can be dismissed as an intentional device used to strengthen its nihilistic message—a protest against the casual commodification of the USSR, one of the states that might at any moment trigger apocalypse.

Neue deutsche Welle artists incorporated space into their music in a variety of ways. Drawing on Cold War tensions, they advocated for a demilitarized cosmos and protested war. They painted an idealized picture of spaceflight and astronauts, despite the dangers of space exploration. Subgenres like alien songs made use of space to dramatic effect. All these types of space songs express uniquely German anxieties over being on the front line of the Cold War, hopes of space as a field for technological advancement and domestic industrial restoration, and positive attitudes toward the foreign, foreigners, and collective humanity in the postwar era. Some of these songs even discuss specific programs that Germany led or took part in, like America's Strategic Defense Initiative or the European Space Agency's Spacelab. However, these songs may be more alike in the topics they neglect than the ones they address. Never is any mention made of the German father of spaceflight rocketry, Wernher von Braun, a Nazi Party member who used concentration camps to manufacture rockets, or the crucial role of Nazi military initiatives in developing the rockets and training the scientists that would one day go on to be essential to (and, indeed, personally recruited by) American and Soviet spaceflight programs. This information was even public knowledge at the time, but von Braun nonetheless remained a popular figure in West Germany— several movies were made about or inspired by him. Clearly, then, for all that neue deutsche Welle artists engaged in a rich discussion of space as a key cultural-political touchstone of the Cold War, there were finite limits on the extent to which the intergenerational German reckoning vis-à-vis Naziism could be hashed out in popular culture.

4 The Crest of the Wave

Just as quickly as neue deutsche Welle emerged, the genre began to evolve again. If early, avant-garde, punk-inspired NDW artists had emerged from "gray city walls," they were moving into high-tech metropolises of the future. Starting as early as 1980, the NDW sound and image began to change, becoming less lo-fi, DIY, and artsy, and adopting more and more trappings of pop music. The November editorial of that year's *Sounds* warned that over the period of only "a few months" the new wave scene (both internationally and within the confines of neue deutsche Welle) had gone from being flush with independent, innovative releases to overrun with a "flood" of "lower-quality" records that are interested primarily in following "trends" or marketing themselves with "promotional gags," such as the use of humor or the (ab)use of thematic clichés like "plastic, robots/technology, [and] concrete." All this, the author argued, resulted in "the sanding away of exactly the corners and edges" that had previously "impeded the easy integration of neue deutsche Welle into traditional record production."[1] Another *Sounds* writer argued in May 1982 that the hope for a truly independent "not-for-profit . . . not career-addicted pop music" that had seemed

---

[1] Joachim Stender, "Musik zwischen Anpassung und Überwindung," SOUNDS Diskurs, *Sounds*, November 1980, 44–5.

possible in 1977 had been proven a naive dream, with neue deutsche Welle becoming highly commercialized and profit-driven.[2] In July, Hilsberg himself, writing with musician and manager Jäki Eldorado under the provocative pseudonyms "Gröfaz and Goldmann" (the former a reference to Adolf Hitler, the latter a stereotypically Jewish surname), called for a "general strike" against and boycott of neue deutsche Welle, claiming that it had become commercialized to the point that not even supposedly independent ventures (which would, hypocritically, include Hilsberg's own ZickZack label) were free of market interests.[3]

These assertions are not inaccurate. Hallmarks of neue deutsche Welle were becoming stylish, approachable trends in popular music. For example, the use of synthesizers and drum machines not only increased; the significance of these instruments was also transformed. Initially, they had represented the displacement of humans by strange, new technologies that were incomprehensible to the average listener. Now, computers were the musician's friend, making her job easier or even helping her find love, as in Paso Doble's 1984 single "Computerliebe" (not to be confused with Kraftwerk's 1981 song of the same name, which conversely describes technology-fueled loneliness). This change coincided with a rise in poppy, danceable hits with aspirational themes. Travel and leisure time featured in pop

---

[2] Anon. "Gibt es noch unabhängige Neue Musik?" *Sounds*, May 1982, 22. The author of this article was left anonymous by the editorial board.
[3] Gröfaz and Goldmann, "Pamphlet," *Sounds*, July 1982, 44. Their identities are confirmed in Rüdiger Esch, *Electri_city: The Düsseldorf School of Electronic Music* (London: Omnibus Press, 2016), 303.

hits, such as Niko's "Am Weißen Strand von Helgoland" ("On the White Beachs of Helgoland"), Snäp!'s "Sommer Sonne Sand und Meer" ("Summer, Sun, Sand, and Sea"), and UKW's "Sommersprossen" ("Freckles"). Industrial noise influences faded into the background as simple beats and melodies rose to the forefront.

The commercialization of a genre, and its associated way of life and political leanings, by the mainstream didn't just represent the idea of "selling out." If one no longer had to be well-versed in the social codes and intellectual framework of the scene to understand or enjoy NDW, then not only was the cultural prestige of the genre diminished, but there also existed a genuine threat to the subcultural community that had sprung up around NDW music, a community that, in many ways, provided an alternative mode of life, outside mainstream German society, to people who found normative lifestyles restrictive. Commercialization could be considered an effective counterattack by the German mainstream against not only an effective cultural alternative but a financial competitor as well.

In a three-part series in late 1980, *Sounds* profiled the "entrepreneurs" behind the alternative media structure, including Hilsberg; Klaus Maeck, who ran Rip Off, a punk record store and distributor in Hamburg; Hollow Skai of No Fun Records; and Burkhard Seiler, the owner of the Zensor record shop in Berlin.[4] The third and final entry in the series

---

[4]Michael O. R. Kröher, "Untergrund und Unternehmer (Teil 1)," *Sounds*, September 1980, 48–51; Diedrich Diederichsen, "Untergrund und Unternehmer (Teil 2)," *Sounds*, November 1980, 54–5.

documents a meeting of eight members of the Düsseldorf "Macherszene" ("doer-scene") from the Ata Tak, Warning Records, and Rondo labels in which they discuss a new joint distributor venture. The question of whether to distribute a new release using a mainstream wholesaler (in the hopes that it might have a broader reach) or sell only through independent record shops was central to the meeting.[5] In all three articles, these so-called "doers" emphasize that they themselves were not making money off of their projects, but that some form of organized business was necessary to support even a seemingly independent scene. This means that notions of the commercial and the underground are inherently flexible. To some readers of *Sounds*, the fact that Hilsberg wrote about bands signed to ZickZack in his own magazine was already an inauthentic conflict of interest. However, interconnected ventures such as these can in equal measure be considered an independent, alternative media structure, centered around NDW. To the extent that this structure was then linked to the art world as well, the possibility for a creatively minded person to establish themselves and live outside the German mainstream grew exponentially.

It should be little surprise that, in order to preempt this alternative, within a few years, mainstream, domestic German media forces began producing neue deutsche Welle artists and flooding the radio and hit parades with their music. International media groups also got in on the trend. The three most prominent major commercial labels releasing neue

---

[5]Michael O. R. Kröher, "Untergrund und Unternehmer Teil 3 und Schluß," *Sounds*, December 1980, 22–4.

deutsche Welle in the 1980s were WEA, CBS, and EMI. WEA Records was the name of Warner Music Group's European distribution arm. Based in New York City, Warner made several aggressive moves in the German music market in the 1980s. An attempted merger with the Dutch-German label PolyGram was stopped by the US Federal Trade Commission in 1984, but in 1988 WEA successfully acquired the Hamburg-based label TELDEC.[6] Operating in West Germany as CBS Schallplatten GmbH, CBS Records distributed music as the subsidiary of the American Columbia Broadcasting System, a media conglomerate that grew out of television and radio broadcasting.[7] Structurally, its music production and distribution arms functioned as an attempt to create an international vertical monopoly. EMI (originally short for Electric and Musical Industries), represented domestically as EMI Electrola GmbH, was a British technology conglomerate. In 1980, EMI acquired the independent West German label Welt-Rekord, founded by Fehlfarben member Peter Hein, but its own parent company is even more interesting. From 1979 to 1996, EMI was merged with the British electrical engineering company Thorn Electrical Industries to form Thorn EMI. One of Thorn EMI's main outputs was military technology, including missile systems; as a contractor, the company had "SDI potential."[8] Major record companies operating in

---

[6]"Warner and Polygram Drop Proposed Merger," *New York Times*, November 7, 1984, 1.

[7]"GmbH" stands for "Gesellschaft mit beschränkter Haftung," meaning "company with limited liability," essentially an LLC.

[8]Edward Reiss, *The Strategic Defense Initiative*, Cambridge Studies in International Relations (Cambridge: Cambridge University Press, 1992), 126.

the German-language market were not only predatory and monopolistic; they also benefited from the very Cold War tensions that endangered (both East and West) Germans.

When it came to the rising popularity of pop-influenced NDW (or NDW-influenced pop), there was an overwhelming preoccupation with the listening habits of young people, paternalistically referred to as "kids." Young people were seen as more malleable and susceptible to cheap marketing tricks. They were supposedly more image-driven, susceptible to advertising, and (especially girls) likely to follow an artist because they found him attractive, rather than actually liking his music. Young listeners did not go quietly. *Sounds* rebutted the notion that "pop music is music for children," arguing that "there is in everyone a child. Therefore it follows that music must also be made for big kids," that is, adults.[9] In the November 1979 issue of *Sounds*, one teenage girl wrote a tongue-in-cheek letter to the editor, requesting more coverage of "songwriters," claiming that punk and new wave music not to her taste. Humorously blaming her underdeveloped preferences on her "paltry little 17 years," the writer claimed she was "too impatient" to wait for the "maturation process" to give her more refined listening habits.[10] The December issue contained even more debate over *Sounds'* new editorial direction. Some readers were pleased that the magazine was bringing attention to the budding neue deutsche Welle scene, viewing it as a productive, culturally rich musical development

---

[9] Michael O. R. Kröher, "Die Doraus BLUMEN UND NARZISSEN Ata Tak WR 12," *Sounds*, March 1982, 57.
[10] Eva Bigalke, "SOUNDS—Die Reifeprüfung?" Leserbriefe, *Sounds*, November 1979, 4.

that was rapidly coming to outshine "the lameness of old rockers." Others disagreed, accusing *Sounds* of not being critical of new wave music. They often lumped punk, new wave, and disco together, contraposing them with rock music, defending their "snooze records" against the "decadent and absolutely merchandised" new wave.[11]

The role of young people in the neue deutsche Welle scene remained a point of tension for two reasons. First, the young, postwar generation of West Germany was an important consumer demographic. Hardcore NDW fans could revile hit parades for shamelessly appealing to the youth taste, but that was their audience too. Some of *Sounds* magazine's most frequent advertisements included anti-pimple products, cigarette and beer pictorials full of smiling young people, and banking services targeting first-time customers. The teen demographic was key across the entire music market.

Finally, distinct from pop-influenced NDW, we can identify music that plays with childish lyrics, singsongy melodies, and participatory rhythms as evocative of children's nursery rhymes. This music may seem superficially childish, but its tropes were often used to ironic effect by independent neue deutsche Welle artists, who drew attention to their absurdity or counterposed them with dark lyrics. For example, in their 1982 song "Keine Probleme Marlene" ("No Problem Marlene") the band Clit repeatedly use first names in order to create childish rhyme schemes; however, the use of an ominous guitar and bass line, as well as a keyboard part that resembles the drone of an alarm, and the repetition of the lyrics "no future, no future" in the chorus

---

[11] Leserbriefe, *Sounds*, December 1979, 4.

make the song seem avant-garde. Dennis Und Die Wilde 13's 1982 single "Schule, Nein Danke!" ("School, No Thanks!") uses child singers but undercuts them by incorporating a sparse drum machine and distortion to satirical effect. This phenomenon also occurred in reverse. Claus Mathias-Clamath's 1982 song "Bin ich niemand" ("I Am No One") could be lyrically read as a nihilistic no-future anthem, but its pop-ballad production and Mathias-Clamath's floppy-haired, clean-cut styling mean that it is read much more commercially. The later years of neue deutsche Welle tend to get painted with a broad brush. They are seen as a descent into substanceless pop music. The pop turn in neue deutsche Welle, while it did give rise to contrived imitation acts, also heralded the appearance of many clever, passionate artists who saw no reason why substantive music could not also be popular, danceable, or commercially successful.

The prototypical example of the thinking man's pop artist is Andreas Dorau. Dorau is interesting on several levels. First, he serves as a link to the "kids sound." Dorau, shockingly, was only fifteen when he recorded his aforementioned smash hit, "Fred vom Jupiter;" *Sounds* jokingly called his 1981 single "Der Lachende Papst" ("The Laughing Pope") the "children's record of the month."[12] While Dorau was a literal teenager, it is more accurate to term him a wunderkind savant than a teen idol. Dorau was also steeped in the independent NDW scene from a young age. He learned to play guitar from Palais Schaumburg member Holger Hiller and was quickly signed to the independent Ata Tak label.[13] At Ata Tak, he worked on

---

[12]Werner Jacobs, *Sounds*, March 1981, 9.
[13]Kid P., "Die Wahrheit über Hamburg!" *Sounds*, May 1985, 26.

avant-garde projects, including a short new media, operatic interpretation of Dadaist texts called "Guten Morgen Hose" ("Good Morning Pants") that he created with Hiller in 1984. It was both the power of these associations and the tongue-in-cheek tone of his lyrics that afforded Dorau a space in the independent neue deutsche Welle scene, even as his songs became hits. For example, a song like "Lokomotivführer" ("Train Driver"), released in 1981, on which Dorau opines about his desire to work as a train driver, could quite literally be played for children. The sheer, infantile absurdity, underscored by Dorau's own age, highlights the irony of the song and helps it transcend nursery rhyme pop. Dorau also uses the contraposition of childlike themes with no future references in "Einkauf" ("Shopping," also 1981), a song in which he describes all his family members going to the market to do their shopping— except him, because he has no money. The 1983 release "Die Welt ist schlecht" ("The World Is Bad") likewise contrasts an upbeat melody with nihilistic lyrics. As time went on, Dorau's music evolved. His production techniques and songwriting stayed poppy, with plentiful synthesizer and backing vocals, but they grew in sophistication as technology improved and Dorau grew as a songwriter. In his song "Demokratie" ("Democracy"), Dorau combines innovative techniques like sampling with a more explicit political message, bemoaning the somehow stagnant, yet contentious, nature of democracy before contending that it is the best of a set of bad options. "Demokratie" was released in 1988 (very generously) at the tail end of NDW. Dorau continued (even into the 1990s) to make pop-influenced neue deutsche Welle music, showing his genuine commitment to the thoughtful use of more approachable songwriting motifs, which in turn allows his music to stand the test of time.

Another group able to walk the pop-independent line was the band Lusthansa. Originally from Trier, their name is a pun on the German airline "Lufthansa," which can roughly be translated to "lusty airline." Accordingly, the band's typography and logo mimic that of the airline, only the icon of a singular bird inside a circle is replaced by two birds, copulating. Lusthansa were not especially prolific, but their 1982 hit "Nix neues in Poona" ("Nothing New in Poona") is a brilliant example of self-aware, politically inflected, pop-influenced neue deutsche Welle. Set to a danceable beat and friendly chords, and with a repetitive chorus, "Nix neues in Poona" sounds like a simple radio hit. The song's lyrics are critical of not only broader social movements but also, subtly, the NDW scene itself. The song is in part a send-up of the Rajneesh movement, a Buddhist organization, popular internationally in the 1970s, that became disgraced after some of its members were involved in a 1984 bioterrorism attack in the United States. "Nix neues in Poona" opens with a stereotypical gong noise and a chant-like intonation, and the band often performed the song in orange jumpsuits, a nod to the garb of the Rajneesh movement, whose members were dubbed "Orange People." The broader intent of the song is to criticize trend-hoppers who pretend to be "free thinkers." "Nix neues in Poona" therefore can also function as a subtle critique of the broader NDW scene as well—an argument against affectation and for an uninhibited style of neue deutsche Welle that was not preoccupied with its avant-garde bona fides or pop success.

Another NDW artist who was able to moderate the incorporation of pop motifs into his work was Joachim Witt. Witt's career does not follow a simple trajectory. Hailing from Hamburg, Witt played in several bands during the 1970s before breaking out on his own as a neue deutsche Welle solo artist. He was never an independent artist, instead signing with WEA. Witt became a star with his first album, *Silberblick*, released in 1980, and its lead single, "Goldener Reiter" ("Golden Rider"). Though the song was a commercial success, rising to second place on the German charts, it is quite sophisticated. While the song is catchy, it is not up-tempo or danceable. It is steady, melodic, and not apparently happy or sad. The lyrics are abstract, describing the flight of the titular golden rider through a city (unnamed, though Witt alludes to the Berlin Wall), as he makes his way to his new home in a psychiatric ward. Darker themes pervade this pop hit; in more recent years, Witt has said that *Silberblick* as an album is a critique of society, and "Goldener Reiter" in particular displays the emptiness of "wealth" and "abundance."[14] In this respect, Witt could be critical of commerciality, even as he went on to release a steady stream of albums (including one in English) and acted in several movies. Even the avant-garde NDW musician and journalist Xao Seffcheque, in his review of *Silberblick*, made an honest attempt to like the album, though he ultimately found it fell short of truly experimental music.[15] In a later issue, Witt claimed he received interest in his music from ZickZack before signing to WEA and stated that he believed

---

[14] "Joachim Witt reagiert auf 'Goldener Reiter,'" *DIFFUS*, October 5, 2022, https://www.youtube.com/watch?v=Ny3S6yX78kQ.

[15] Xao Seffcheque, "Joachim Witt: SILBERBLICK, WEA 58.231," Platten, *Sounds*, January 1981, 60–1.

independent labels were "important," especially for musicians who had not been able to break into the industry through mainstream avenues.[16] Witt is a prime example of how NDW artists could produce pop music while remaining self-aware. Not all pop-influenced NDW was substanceless or devoid of connection to the genre's history.

This is not to say that the phenomenon of "bad" neue deutsche Welle was a fiction. A glut of artists cashed in on the sound of the genre but replaced its social critiques with shallow messages and nonsense lyrics. This music reflected broader trends in pop-influenced new wave music in the 1980s. Resultantly, the neue deutsche Welle music that will be discussed in this section is some of the least distinctly German music produced under the genre designation.

Before talking about some more specific examples, it is worthwhile to discuss a bigger trend in commercial NDW: the use of English, specifically in an attempt to break into global markets. The use of English in the lyrics of a song alone does not automatically denote an artist who is attempting to "sell out" or "break America" (or, more likely, Britain, or even just western Europe); it was not at all uncommon for early neue deutsche Welle bands to sing songs in English. For example, the early Austrian punk band Chuzpe used English on their first single in 1979. This move was not a means to appeal to a foreign market; it was an indication of the influence that English-speaking bands had had on the group (Chuzpe released a cover of Joy Division's "Love Will Tear Us Apart" in 1980). Many early NDW bands got their start just like most musicians, singing covers of songs by

---

[16] Michael O. R. Kröher, "Joachim Witt: Keine Kuhhändel," *Sounds*, April 1981, 20.

their own favorite artists. Since the German-language scene was undefined at the time, naturally, those artists' songs would have been in English, creating an early, default association between the English language and the new wave sound. Die Gesunden (a band with many connections to Einstürzende Neubauten), Insisters, Malaria!, and Materialschlacht (which had a Fehlfarben connection) are all good examples of early, lo-fi or experimental neue deutsche Welle groups that sang in English. A lesser phenomenon is exemplified by Xmal Deutschland and Liliput, two bands that signed to prominent independent labels based in the UK—4AD and Rough Trade, respectively—and released music there in English. In a few instances, it was possible to break into the English-language market via independent cultural networks, but this was far from the norm.

When the language shift was reversed, and an NDW artist who had originally sung in German began to produce work in English, it almost always corresponded with an increasingly commercialized sound. For example, the duo Ti-Tho released a few more experimental singles on ZickZack, but after signing to Polydor they put out English-language pop hits. The Group Ja Ja Ja, who made passable neue deutsche Welle before switching to sing in English, saw a dramatic decrease in the quality of their lyrics and a strange incorporation of hip-hop influences with a grating brand of theatricality. Peter Schilling, whose famous cover of David Bowie's "Major Tom" was discussed above, also recorded a version of the cover, as well as a number of original songs, in English, likely in a continued attempt to use crossover appeal to his advantage. Some bands, like Fred Banana Combo, sang (almost) entirely in English for the duration of their careers.

NDW artists did not need to change the language of their music to "sell out." There was a thriving market for commercial new wave music in Germany. For example, the soloist Markus had a number of successful singles in the early 1980s. In 1982, Markus released "Ich will Spaß" ("I Want Fun") off of his debut album *Kugelblitze & Raketen* (*"Ball Lightning and Rockets"*), in which he sings about his desire to be young, have fun, and drive fast. We can generously interpret some ironic notes in Markus' music. On the final refrain of "Ich will Spaß," he calls out to all of Germany, asking if they can hear him and enticing their participation in his jubilation. For the *ZDF-Hitparade* performance of "Ich will Spaß," Markus wore socks with sandals and bounced around waving a German flag, behavior so over-the-top it had to be marginally self-aware. Nonetheless, enticing audience participation on hit parade shows hardly approaches true social critique. *Kugelblitze & Raketen* was dubbed "neue deutsche Schlager" by its *Sounds* reviewer, who did admit that it was sonically progressive (for pop music), if thematically staid.[17] The album title can also be read ironically; it contraposes two types of light that might come from above, ball lightning—a weather phenomenon—and rockets, one natural and (more or less) harmless, the other man-made with the potential to cause armageddon. This juxtaposition may seem like a reference to "99 Luftballons," but *Kugelblitze & Raketen* was released a year before Nena's smash hit.[18]

---

[17] Franziska D. Graf, "Markus KUGELBLITZE UND RAKETEN CBS 85 732," *Sounds*, June 1982, 70–1.
[18] Nena and Markus did collaborate on a version of the single "Kleine Taschenlampe brenn'" ("A Little Flashlight Shines") in 1983. Both artists were signed to CBS at the time.

Another group known for their pop hits, but whose work still exhibits some unique characteristics, is Spider Murphy Gang. They are best remembered for their 1981 hit "Skandal im Sperrbezirk" ("Scandal in the Restricted Area"), which tells the story of a popular sex worker, Rosi, who is taking clients outside the designated zones in which prostitution is allowed (i.e., in the restricted area, an area of Munich which was dramatically enlarged, first upon the occasion of the 1972 Olympics and then several more times throughout the 1980s). While this local reference, as well as the fact that the band often incorporated the Bavarian dialect into their music (a behavior also exhibited by the pop NDW group Relax), made it unique and resistant to homogenization, "Skandal im Sperrbezirk" is ultimately a good-time party song that hit number 1 on the German charts.

One final, prominent example of commercial neue deutsche Welle is the group Münchener Freiheit, named after Liberty Square in Munich. Also a CBS artist, they released six albums over the course of the 1980s, all of them full of synth-heavy, power pop-inspired love songs. Deeply devotional, saccharine, and admittedly catchy, there is not a shred of irony in Münchener Freiheit's catalog. Songs like "Ohne Dich (Schlaf' Ich Heut Nacht Nicht Ein)" ("Without You (I Can't Go to Sleep Tonight"), "Tausendmal Du" ("One Thousand Times You"), and "Herzschlag Ist der Takt" ("Heartbeat Is the Rhythm") describe being in love and enthralled with on one's romantic partner. Münchener Freiheit would continue to put out records well into the 2010s and, in the pinnacle of camp sensibility (complete earnestness to the point of absurdity), represented Germany at the Eurovision Song Contest in 1993, placing eighteenth out of twenty-five participating countries.

The commercial turn in neue deutsche Welle was more than just a shift in the genre that saw a greater volume of pop-influenced music released on larger labels. Indeed, if underground neue deutsche Welle provided an alternative lifestyle from the mainstream, then commercial NDW was that mainstream and likewise exemplified a lifestyle of its own. Accordingly, this was more than a genre shift; it was the creation of a mode of being. Aside from just listening to the latest neue deutsche Welle hits, commercial forces sought to make crossover movie stars out of the biggest faces of NDW, and vice versa, to turn movie stars into NDW artists. There are two significant examples of this phenomenon. The first is the 1983 movie *Gib Gas – Ich Will Spaß* ("*Step on the Gas, I Want Fun*"), a jukebox musical starring Markus and Nena, in which, over the course of an international pursuit across Europe, Markus wins Nena over with his charms and driving ability. *Gib Gas – Ich Will Spaß* incorporates many of the two artists' songs into the plot, its leads lip-synching along. The film was a moderate domestic success at the box office but met with near universally poor reviews. For Markus, who had already had his big hit song, *Gib Gas – Ich Will Spaß* seemed to cement his mainstream idol status and indicate his crossover star ambitions. Nena differed in that she was not a solo artist, but rather the front woman of her eponymous band, which, while it had had success with the single "Nur geträumt" ("Only Dreamed"), had not yet broken through with "99 Luftballons." Nena would come to regret taking part in *Gib Gas – Ich Will Spaß*. One NME article calls it a "bad teen exploitation movie" that nonetheless gave the band their first breakthrough, relating a plea from Nena to never "talk about this fucking movie . . . I hate it. It follows me wherever we go!"[19]

The other film of the neue deutsche Welle scene was released two years earlier, in 1981. Titled *Christiane F. – Wir Kinder vom Bahnhof Zoo* ("*Christiane F. – We the Children of the Zoo Train Station*"), the film is much darker than *Gib Gas – Ich Will Spaß*. It follows the titular Christiane, a thirteen-year-old girl living in West Berlin in the 1970s, as she runs away from home and gets caught up in drug addiction and prostitution. Despite the fact that the actors themselves were underage, they were allowed to participate in graphic scenes depicting nudity, intercourse, and drug abuse. The film is also notable for the involvement of David Bowie, who both played himself, giving a concert, and contributed to the soundtrack. Due both to the time period it is set in and the predominance of an English star, it is difficult to say that *Christiane F.* is representative of the neue deutsche Welle scene. It depicts the social conditions (lack of a safety net and safe spaces for young people to socialize) in West Germany that gave rise to the NDW community.

The film's connections to the neue deutsche Welle scene come after the fact—it launched the music career of the real Christiane F. (full name Vera Christiane Felscherinow). The movie *Christiane F.* was based off of her autobiography, published in 1978. Rather than attempt to make the actress, Natja Brunckhorst, who portrayed Christiane in the film, into a pop star, it was the real Christiane who capitalized on the release to launch her music career. The rise of Felscherinow's music career was not entirely contrived, as she was in a

---

[19] Biba Kopf, "Nena: The Girl from C&A," *New Musical Express*, May 5, 1984.

relationship with Alexander Hacke, a member of Einstürzende Neubauten, at the time, and had connections to the respected underground NDW scene. She only released a couple of singles, both in 1982 on small labels. The music was dark and featured both English and German lyrics, characteristic of the film's connections to the British new wave scene via David Bowie and the desire to draw upon the broader audience that he could confer.

In addition to film, television also played an important part in the formation of a totalizing neue deutsche Welle scene. This worked on two levels. First, similar to America, the presence of music videos on television was becoming crucial to the music market in Germany. The television program *Der Musikladen* ("*The Music Shop*") produced by Radio Bremen, for example, interspersed music videos with live artist performances. This was a large part of how newer, more commercial artists got their edge over underground ones: their record labels could afford to produce music videos and, no matter how trite they were, the simple fact that they existed gave those artists a better chance for exposure via music video replay shows—including in America, on MTV. Nena recorded a promotional sting for the network in 1984, and Falco hosted his own guest VJ program in 1986. Hit parades, specifically *ZDF-Hitparade*, became crucial for the promotion of pop-influenced neue deutsche Welle acts in the early 1980s. More characteristic of European markets, the hit parade format involves a chart countdown of the top-ranking artists (usually that week), in which a number of said bands (or solo acts) come to the television studio and perform their hit in front of a live audience of fans. The performances, which were done live, used either half or full playback. In this respect, the *ZDF-Hitparade* is less an artifice of the popular, promotional circuit than some of its foreign equivalents (see, for example, the British show *Top of the Pops*).

The more serious medium through which fans engaged with the NDW scene was magazines, though even these varied in quality. There was the aforementioned *Sounds* magazine, which was well-regarded, with a long-standing history as an independent, countercultural publication. *Sounds* was purchased by and amalgamated into the German *New Music Express* in 1981, from which point it became a more typical, popular music magazine. Around this time another independent magazine, *SPEX*, emerged. It had a longer shelf life in large part because it turned to hip-hop and later indie rock, as NDW fell out of vogue, but was never as cutting edge as *Sounds*. Fanzines were also a part of the neue deutsche Welle scene, including Jürgen Kramer's *Die 80er Jahre* ("*The 80s*"), the Bonn-based *Datenverarbeitung* ("*Data Processing*"), and *Heimatblatt* ("*Homeland Gazette*") from Düsseldorf. *Sounds* would also regularly publish the mailing addresses of fanzines in its "Neuestes Deutschlands" ("Germany's Newest") section. Additionally, the 1984 documentary film *So war das S.O. 36* ("*That's How the S.O. 36 [Nightclub] Was*"), directed by Manfred O. Jelinski and Jörg Buttgereit, documented the West Berlin scene of the early 1980s, using the SO36 nightclub as a frame of reference.

The commercial "total NDW" scene of pop music, film, and television was by no means isolated from the independent neue deutsche Welle scene. The first, prototypical example is the band Nena and their aforementioned hit, "99 Luftballons." As discussed, this NDW mega-hit, which went on to become popular around the world in its original German, even before the band rerecorded it in English, had a very sophisticated message about the Cold War and the potential for high-level, faceless government warmongers to drag an unwilling populace into armageddon. Other examples abound. Geier Sturzflug scored a hit with their song "Bruttosozialprodukt" ("Gross National Product"). At even the highest level of commercial success, neue deutsche Welle was a genre that afforded political messaging space to articulate complex narratives.

For example, the 1983 song "Karl der Käfer" ("Karl the Beetle"), by the Cologne band Gänsehaut, is an example of a commercially successful song with a political message. The song tells the story of the titular Karl, a beetle who finds himself homeless due to deforestation. It was a hit on the German charts and performed on hit parades as well. "Karl der Käfer" and "99 Luftballons" are an illustrative duo because of the trajectory of their respective bands. While Nena had several other hits (none of them political) before fizzling out, Gänsehaut was an environmentalist act through-and-through, and none of their other songs were breakout hits. It is possible that being politically minded functioned as something of a gimmick, capable of producing popular success but not long-lasting consciousness.

The best way to articulate the crossover between independent and commercial neue deutsche Welle is not to track ideas or political beliefs but to follow the career trajectories of individual musicians. The NDW scene is replete with artists who oscillated between different bands and solo projects, often taking part in multiple efforts at once. The best example of individuals who crossed over between the two main "sounds" of NDW are the Humpe sisters, Annette and Inga. The sisters got their start as vocalists in Neonbabies, an early NDW band known for their more avant-garde sound, incorporating vocal effects, amateur singing, and plentiful use of horns. Their 1983 single "Eiskalter Engel" ("Ice Cold Angel") is an excellent example of the innovative use of the German language by neue deutsche Welle artists. Contemporaneously, the sisters were also a part of the band Ideal, which straddled the line between independent and commercial acts. While they had political songs, such as "Keine Heimat" ("No Homeland"), which criticizes the United States, and the anti-consumerist "Luxus" ("Luxury"), the band is most well-remembered for their big hit "Blaue Augen" ("Blue Eyes"), a song about being love-struck by a boy with blue eyes. "Blaue Augen" was originally a Neonbabies song, but the less avant-garde rerecording by Ideal was the version that became a hit. From there, the Humpe sisters moved to more behind-the-scenes roles for a time. Annette worked as a songwriter and producer on the aforementioned track "Codo," while Inga was a backing singer and member of the band DÖF. While "Codo" was a pop hit, DÖF itself was a very self-aware project that took many cues from performance art and sought to lampoon the broader neue deutsche Welle scene. Its name, which stands for Deutsch-Österreichisches Feingefühl ("German-Austrian Tactfulness"), is a parody of the band DAF (Deutsch Amerikanische Freundschaft, or "German-American Friendship"). "Codo" itself was a parody of other contemporary space songs; the melody is borrowed from the East German hit "Küss mich und lieb mich" ("Kiss Me and Love Me") written by Holger Biege, who sued DÖF for plagiarism.

Continuing this work, both sisters became producers for the band Palais Schaumberg. Annette also worked as a producer with Udo Lindenberg, die Prinzen, and Nena, and provided backing vocals for the band Trio. Inga was a guest singer for Falco. In the mid-1980s, the sisters turned to pop. They began making music as a duo, referred to as Humpe (und) Humpe in German-language markets and Swimming with Sharks in English-language ones. Their releases together in this decade were commercial neue deutsche Welle. The songs, which used English as often as they did German, were simplistic and discussed love and relationships. This project was a clear attempt to capitalize on the broader popularity of the new wave sound and break into international markets. The sisters were not simply the face of the act, as they also continued their songwriting and production duties. Despite moderate domestic success, this project fizzled out, and Annette and Inga returned to more behind-the-scenes roles in smaller, independent projects.

The narrative of a "true" or "authentic" independent neue deutsche Welle scene that arose in 1980 and 1981, only to rapidly be taken over and appropriated by the commercial juggernaut of pop-music media in 1982, such that by 1984 the scene was dead, is not accurate. Within a time period as tight as 1980–4, not even a decade long, it is impossible to periodize artistic movements. Independently minded artists, including the bands Extrabreit and Freiwillige Selbstkontrolle, working with established tropes of industrial noise or minimal synth, continued to produce music through the end of the 1980s and beyond. And while many of these artists were original, there were an equal number that used these musical signposts to signal originality when, in fact, they were derivative of the sound and "no future" themes that came before them. Equally, pop-influenced NDW was an important part of the genre from its early days. While it is undeniable that many acts on large record labels adopted upbeat synths and dance beats as a way of capitalizing on the sound of the day, not all of these commercial artists were making substanceless music. For example, the band Rheingold released innovative music on large, commercial labels, such as EMI and CBS, and groups with a more pop sound, like die Zimmermänner and Große Freiheit, appeared on independent labels. In that sense, while we can identify two major trends in the sound of NDW music, the notion that there was a clear divide between an "authentic" scene and a "fake" one is a fiction—artistic independence and commerciality manifested as a spectrum which artists often moved back and forth on as their careers progressed.

5 The "Other" Neue Deutsche Welle

Falco and the Austrian Scene

The word "German" in "neue deutsche Welle" refers to language, not nationality. As has been demonstrated, NDW existed on both sides of the Iron Curtain, in both the Federal Republic of Germany and the German Democratic Republic. It stands to reason, then, that the wave would come to the shores of other German-speaking countries, namely, Austria and Switzerland.

In the Austrian context, Vienna was the natural hub. Vienna had something of a conservative reputation, with one journalist calling it "straight-laced" and another remarking that though "the streets . . . appear to have been vacuumed" and "it is extremely beautiful," he "wouldn't like to live there." Vienna was in a sense *too* perfect. Its old-world magnificence was classically stunning, but the city lacked an edge.[1] Still, most Austrian groups played music indistinguishable from their German counterparts. The band Blümchen Blau had a sparse sound, evocative of early British pioneers like Wire, and exhibited an innovative use of German. Xao Seffcheque

---

[1] Jeffrey Morgan, "Siouxsie and the Banshees: A Kiss in the Dreamhouse (Polydor)," unpublished, 1982, Rock's Backpages Archive. See also Robin Banks, "Clash at the Apocalypse Hotel," *ZigZag*, November 1981.

was an avant-garde synth artist and music critic. Minisex, who scored hits with a few narratively simple pop songs, are a great example of the commercial turn in NDW. Even a group like Edelweiss, which foregrounded kitschy Austrian tropes, produced music that is indistinguishable from any other late-neue deutsche Welle, early-Eurodance artist.

There is one major exception to this rule: Falco. Born Johann Hölzel in 1957, Falco is his country's most well-known musical export since Mozart. His music can best be described as neue deutsche Welle, due to its combination of pop aesthetics, rap lyrical delivery, electronic instruments, and classical samples. Falco foregrounds not only the city of Vienna but also the broader history of the Austro-Hungarian Empire, in order to create his own, distinctly Austrian niche in neue deutsche Welle. Though Falco was born almost fifty years after the empire's dissolution, his music nonetheless contains strong echoes of its grandest epochs and darkest ages. Falco connects contemporary Austria to the Habsburg dynasty through musical heritage, Viennese identity, ruminations on Austria's national neighbors, and the persistent shadow of empire. These connections all serve to show the strength of imperial memory, an anamnesis so strong it has leaked into fields as remote as popular music.

In one of his biggest hits, "Rock Me Amadeus" (1985), Falco draws a direct connection between himself and court composer Wolfgang Amadeus Mozart, describing Mozart as a "superstar" and a "rock idol." In doing so, Falco places himself in the same category as the composer, implying that they are two of a kind, separated by naught more than two centuries. They share in the experience of fame and popularity that shapes all star musicians. Just like a modern pop star of the 1980s, Mozart was swept up in a whirlwind of popularity. Mazierska agrees, noting that "Rock Me Amadeus" exemplifies how one can connect to the past using a "matrix of the present" composed of a series of contemporary phenomena, in this case the hallmarks of fame and popular music.[2] This network of references allows Falco to situate himself within the storied Habsburg musical tradition.

In the 1986 song "The Sound of Musik," Falco imbues the contemporary neue deutsche Welle sound with ancient naturalistic national myths. Falco paints the image of a people coming out of a forest to begin a tradition of music making. Out of the hot wind of this first wave of primordial compositions came a musical legacy that persists in the rock and punk hits of the present day. Given the title of the song, a reference to the 1965 movie *The Sound of Music*, it can be assumed the musical tradition Falco is referring to is decidedly Austrian. In "The Sound of Musik" Falco describes a people taking inspiration from nature to create their own musical tradition. The mythic nature of this narrative is further substantiated by Mazierska's observation that "The Sound of Musik," because of its chronological dislocation, exists in a state of "unreality."[3] The song's lack of temporal identifiers means it could be taking place in primordial German lands, the Habsburg court, 1980s Austria, or all three at once.

---

[2] Ewa Mazierska, "Tourism and Heterotopia in Falco's Songs," in *Relocating Popular Music*, ed. Mazierska and Georgina Gregory (New York: Palgrave MacMillan, 2015), 177.
[3] Ibid., 171.

Another frequent subject of Falco's music is the city of Vienna. Falco characterizes his city as having a frenetic, almost violent energy. In the chorus of his 1988 song "Wiener Blut" ("Viennese Blood"), Falco sings about the inherent vivacity of Viennese blood, depicting the Viennese as relishing their decadent lifestyle not just in their personal dalliances but as an omnipresent *modus operandi*. While Berlin musicians seem to be singing about a party at the end of the world, Falco's description of Vienna is more festive—opulent and uncomplicated—not burdened by any hardship of postwar occupation (though Vienna was occupied in a fashion similar to Berlin until 1955). In fact, "Wiener Blut" is better located in the distant past. Mazierska highlights the other "Wiener Blut," an 1873 waltz composed by Johann Strauss II, to make the argument that Falco is implying the existence of a bacchanalian web stretching between contemporary Austria and the infamously gluttonous Habsburg monarchy.[4]

Falco also made this comparison in his 1981 song "Ganz Wien" ("All of Vienna"), reveling in Viennese decadence as he likens Habsburg court excesses to his own drug binges. In this song, he sings about how all of Vienna is taking cocaine, making reference to the "ball season," an aristocratic custom that again connotes the decadence of the Habsburg court. Falco himself was dependent on cocaine, and it was likely a factor in the car crash that took his life in 1998. Mazierska describes drugs in "Ganz Wien" as a "social leveller." She writes that they have the same ostentatious decadence as the old imperial ball season but are much more accessible than

---

[4] Mazierska, *Falco and Beyond*, 104–5.

any aristocratic tradition.[5] In an age of postwar indulgence, everyone can partake in the court fashions of the day—but this easy availability of decadence is different from the more DIY aesthetic of independent NDW.

At times, Falco even seems to see Vienna as a dying metropolis, still vibrant but at the start of a long process of abandonment and obscurification. In "Vienna Calling" (1985), he laments the flight of young socialites from the city, bemoaning the fact that the young Viennese women of yore have fled for greener pastures in America. Adopting a modern *flâneur* personality, he is a tourist at home, "known" by Vienna, yet still baffled by the disappearance of all the young girls who lent his city the spirit of a world cultural capital.[6] This would indicate an opposite trajectory from Berlin. While unoccupied Vienna was coasting on its Habsburg heyday, Berlin was being reinvigorated by the oppression of occupation.

Just as in Berlin, the club was an important institution in Vienna, but the act of clubbing was far less politicized. One prominent institution, U4 Club, was referenced by Falco on "Ganz Wien" and was by the early 1980s the "most fashionable" venue in the city.[7] Clubs like U4 and its contemporary, Chelsea, began as rock venues but by the 1980s were hosting electronic nights as well—demonstrating the beginnings of a transition from punk, rock, and new wave to dance music and electronica in Vienna.[8] As in Berlin, many Viennese clubs were set up in

---

[5] Ibid., 64.
[6] Ibid., 95.
[7] Ewa Mazierska, *Popular Viennese Electronic Music, 1990-2015: A Cultural History* (London: Routledge, 2019), 39.
[8] Ibid., 57.

"recycled spaces," but because Vienna had experienced far less "de-industrialization" it had fewer appropriate postindustrial venues. This resulted in more clubbing in proximity to residential zones, where noise complaints were more frequent and there was less opportunity for gang involvement. A lower incidence of organized crime is a good thing, but it led to the Vienna scene being perceived as "bourgeoise and conformist."[9]

Falco is not limited to Vienna; his music looks to the whole of the Austro-Hungarian Empire as the basis for contemporary Austrian identity. In his 1992 song "Monarchy Now," he questions whether there will always be some kind of monarch figure ruling over Austria. Falco tells the tale of a runaway train of monarchical excess, cheered on by simple country folk who do not realize that their revered leaders bring death and blight upon them, in the form of needless spending and war. Mazierska interprets Falco's lyrics as a tragic tale of "ordinary people's love of their leaders, the leaders' indifference to them and, ultimately, the implication of ordinary people in grand politics."[10] While her assertion that Falco does not look favorably upon the decision-making ability of "ordinary people" is accurate, she places less emphasis on his equal, if not greater, disdain for the great leaders themselves. Falco's music presents the same doomed cycle of reverence and apathy that Mazierska does, a paradigm that one would not be hard-pressed to apply to the Habsburgs, whose entire mandate rested on a familial union, not good governance.

---

[9] Ibid., 58.
[10] Mazierska, *Falco and Beyond*, 124.

One of Falco's most famous songs, "Der Kommissar" (1981), deals with an unidentified *fin-de-siècle* bureaucrat, giving it cross-temporal applications between contemporary Communist regimes and the Habsburg Empire's collapse at the end of the First World War. Though the figure of the commissar is often interpreted to be an East Berlin Stasi officer, Mazierska argues that he can be understood to be more generally "a policeman or any figure of authority," going as far back as the imperial *Kommissare* described in Jaroslav Hašek's seminal Habsburg satire *The Good Soldier Švejk*, which was published serially in the early 1920s. The drug-taking clubgoer of the 1980s is superimposed onto the provincial peasant of the 1920s. Though the commissar Falco describes is someone to be wary of, the song's overall pop mood and the sarcastic tone with which Falco describes the strong officer in comparison to the small, stupid civilians suggests that the fearsome authority figure is, in reality, better understood as an overworked bureaucrat with a quota to fill. As the administration he represents loses its hold on the people, he must dig his nails in deeper, yet he struggles in vain. Such a doomed struggle was not unknown to the Habsburg Empire, specifically as it fell apart after the First World War. Instead of figuring out ways to win the people over and rejuvenate the state, the imperial leadership, like Falco's commissar, focused on binding it together defensively, paranoid of every potential threat.

Falco also looks beyond the boundaries of Austria. As mentioned, he is concerned with the United States as a global Cold War power, but he also reserves some anxiety for Germany. In the 1984 song "No Answer (Hallo Deutschland)," Falco describes calling his friends in West Berlin but not being able to get through to them, whether due to technical malfunction or a more metaphorical miscommunication. While the song is one of Falco's cheesiest efforts, its subject, frustrated Austrian-German communication, has not always been novel. From the outbreak of the Austro-Prussian War in 1866, when Otto von Bismarck effectively dissolved the German Confederation in response to Austria raising the issue of the administration of Schleswig-Holstein, it seemed Austria and Prussia were never on the same page. This miscommunication had the unfortunate and deadly consequence of pitting two "brother" nations against one another. Falco, too, did not seek to stray from his Germanic siblings. Though he had hits in the English-speaking world (most notably "Der Kommissar" and "Rock Me Amadeus"), he remained an avowed German-language artist and never sought to break through or transition to the American market. This was not a matter of wanting to attain global fame and failing but a conscious choice to avoid the superficial, exoticized celebrity exemplified by Falco's frequent comparator (because of their shared nationality), Arnold Schwarzenegger. In this manner, Mazierska suggests that Falco subscribed to the linguist Wilhelm von Humboldt's notion "that there resides in every language a characteristic worldview," or "Volksgeist," and that therefore "Austrians whose gifts are of a more subtle nature" should "remain at home."[11] Falco too struggled with the question of what constitutes a great Austrian. He did not want to become an American nor a German but to express his Austrian identity on his own terms.

[11] Ibid., 39–41.

Falco's music is often concerned with identity during times of political or economic dislocation. In the 1988 song "Tricks," Falco self-referentially addresses nationality in the age of consumerism and ideology. He questions the Viennese identity he once professed to hold so dear, equating established ethno-national identities, such as Hungarian and Bavarian, with the newer, frequently maligned hippie lifestyle. Mazierska sees this as both an evocation and a frustration of "Romantic mythology," as Falco suggests that "in contemporary times the Romantic effect can be manufactured and purchased."[12] One no longer has to subscribe to a national myth; in the globalized, capitalist age there are now consumer-oriented lifestyles that can be tried on and bought like an off-the-rack dress. Austro-Hungarian identity faced a similar challenge, one that led to the downfall of the empire on the eve of the First World War. On this occasion, the Habsburg monarchy and, by extension, the basis for Austrian rule, faced a challenge to its legitimacy by nascent national movements, whose violent expression in the form of the assassination of Archduke Franz Ferdinand entangled the state in a needless war which would lead to the dissolution of the empire. Falco reflects a similar national state of crisis, transposed some seventy years into the future.

Finally, one can see Falco move beyond Habsburg themes, as he turns away from an Austrian identity and toward a European one. Mazierska interprets much of Falco's work through the lens of neoliberalism, with particular attention to the "'heroic' period or 'imperial' phase" of the system in the 1980s.[13] Falco's

---

[12] Ibid., 28.
[13] Ibid., 2.

song "Europa" was released posthumously in 1999, at the peak of the so-called "end of history" and at the height of European Union accessions.[14] Former Communist states were about to join the EU in droves, and a new vision of a united Europe was taking shape. Though the song is not expressly political, Falco defends this vision, warning off not politicians, but a shady chorus line that pushes for national divisions over a united, European whole. This rejection represents the final evolution of the message of the 1955 Federal Constitutional Law on the Neutrality of Austria, wherein it was declared that Austria would maintain absolute military neutrality. Falco vows, too, that Austria will never again seek to impress herself upon other nations, instead choosing to defend a new multinational vision of Europe.

It would be ludicrous, verging on conspiratorial, to suggest that Falco (or the team of producers, songwriters, stylists, and marketers that created "Falco" in collaboration with Johann Hölzel) set out to write a catalog of music that would chronicle the memory of Habsburg identity. One cannot deny that the same motifs—a strong musical tradition, the centrality and individuality of Vienna, the birth of nationality, and the tribulations of empire—which characterized Austria-Hungary, recur in his music. Falco is as much the heir to Austria's legendary court composers as he is a neue deutsche Welle star.

Although it may seem strange in a book discussing "German" new wave to devote the most space afforded to any single artist to an Austrian, there is no West German equivalent to

[14] Francis Fukuyama, "The End of History?" *The National Interest*, Summer, 1989.

Falco. Artists like Kraftwerk, Einstürzende Neubauten, and Nena had outsize effects on neue deutsche Welle as pioneers of the avant-garde sound, as crucial builders of artist networks with relationships to many important bands, or as global populizers of the genre, respectively. While these bands were influenced by the contemporary sociopolitical context of postwar West Germany, none of them reached back to the history of Prussia for creative inspiration or criticized the very concept of the German national myth. None of these artists achieved the same sustained crossover between the underground and the mainstream that Falco did. In a sense, it is impossible to even determine whether Falco himself was an independent or pop artist. Signed to the independent Austrian label GiG Records, Falco nonetheless achieved consistent chart-topping hits across Europe, including five top-ten singles in Switzerland, eleven in West Germany, and seventeen in Austria. "Rock Me Amadeus" even hit #1 in the United States; in total, Falco has sold approximately forty million albums.[15] While his catalog has been commercially abused after his untimely death in 1998 in a substance-fueled car accident in the Dominican Republic, Falco resisted the many opportunities he had to "sell out" during his lifetime and did not capitalize on the international success of his music. He is not a crossover artist but an artist who occupied parallel spaces in the mainstream and the underground. This makes him the purest manifestation of new wave music. If one invokes Haddon's definition of the new

---

[15] Marco Lauer, "Falco: Auf der Flucht vor der Banalität," *Stern*, February 6, 2008, https://www.stern.de/kultur/musik/falco-auf-der-flucht-vor-der-banalitaet-3219086.html.

wave as avant-garde pop music, it becomes reasonable to argue that the most quintessential neue deutsche Welle artist was, in fact, an Austrian.

Switzerland

The Swiss scene is also a worthwhile topic of discussion. Compared to West German and Austrian neue deutsche Welle, Swiss artists remained more isolated from prevailing commercial trends. The Swiss sound could be termed "dark wave," a subset of post-punk and new wave music that trended toward the atonal, bleak, or gothic. For example, the biggest hit to come out of the Swiss scene, the 1981 single "Eisbär" ("Polar Bear"), by the Bern-based band Grauzone, features amateur, plaintive vocals over fuzzy white noise and a jangly rhythm guitar section that at intervals breaks down into abstract noise. Synthesizer provides some additional atmosphere and a caterwauling saxophone solo by Claudine Chirac caps off the song, but it is sparse and characterized by empty spaces that are interrupted by fits of sound. Fittingly, the lyrics discuss a troubled relationship, in which the singer wishes he was a polar bear, because in the cold of the North Pole he would feel nothing and never cry. The music video for "Eisbär" likewise is avant-garde, depicting an emptied-out abstraction of a dance floor. It features two women, dressed in sparkly evening wear, dancing alone in a dark, smoke-filled room. "Eisbär" charted in West Germany and Austria, but commercial success proved to be Grauzone's undoing. They refused to perform the song live, and (in a similar fashion to New Order) their hit single did not appear on their first, self-titled album. The band broke up in 1982, only two years after they had formed.

The original release of "Eisbär" came on a 1980 compilation, *Swiss Wave the Album*, released by the independent Swiss label Off Course Records. Though it was released domestically, the compilation was intended for broader consumption. All of the sleeve text is in English, and only the two songs by Grauzone are sung in German; the other ten are in English. As discussed earlier, in this early phase of neue deutsche Welle, the choice to use English represents a connection to the British post-punk and new wave scene, rather than an intent to "sell out." Regardless, there was a clear attempt to reach broader, English-speaking audiences.

Another group featured on the Swiss wave compilation, whose career followed a similar trajectory, is Liliput. While they have been mentioned before for being composed entirely of women and for their signing to Rough Trade, it is worth talking about Liliput in the context of the Swiss scene. Formed in 1978 in Zürich as Kleenex, Liliput changed their name in 1979 after the threat of legal action from the tissue brand. Possibly the only reason the underground Swiss band came to the attention of the Kimberly-Clark Corporation is because they had been championed by John Peel, though they never recorded a session with him. Liliput fit the mold of the British post-punk girl group; they attracted comparisons to the Raincoats, who they toured with, and the Slits. The first mention of the band in *Sounds* in 1979 stresses their connection to the UK. The article is bookended with references to Liliput's appearance in an (unnamed) English music magazine and on the airwaves of a London radio station. Peel is quoted as describing the band as "one of the freshest, most energetic groups in years." The article notes that Liliput's record is not yet available in Germany, when it is already available in the UK, but the author stresses that the music is sung in "German, and something like English."[16] Liliput's music is indeed lo-fi, swinging between casual irreverence and gut-wrenching sincerity. They adapted the punk attitude, with its focus on aggression and rejection of perfectionism, to the female experience and the new wave sensibility. Their output also has an element of performance art, with the band members adopting stage names and dressing monochromatically to perform. Liliput's core member, the bassist Klaudia Schifferle, went on to become a painter. Liliput broke up in 1983, due in part to the demands of being an underground band and also because their lead vocalist, Astrid Spirit, became pregnant and chose not to tour after giving birth.

While Off Course Records, via their compilation release, has defined much of the present-day understanding of the Swiss scene, other groups exist outside of the label's orbit. For example, Mittageisen. Best translated as "iron for lunch," the band took its name from a 1978 song by Siouxsie and the Banshees, which was itself a tribute to an antifascist photomontage by the German artist John Heartfield, a work of art that mocked a speech by the Nazi leader Hermann Göring. This pattern of exchange is instructive, because it shows just how influential the Swiss scene was on British artists, and vice

---

[16] Marianne Berna, "Kleenex: Heisse Sounds aus dem Schwiizerland," *Sounds*, February, 1979, 8.

versa, displaying a dialogue between the two centers of post-punk and new wave music. Broadly, German aesthetics were often used by British bands to give their music a dark edge. Consider, for example, Joy Division, who took their name from the semi-fictionalized Nazi system of sexual slavery, or Cabaret Voltaire, named for a Zürich nightclub that Heartfield himself was a member of. At the same time, German-speaking bands had their own connections to the British scene. Mittageisen were early adopters of the industrial sound, which they mixed with both Kraftwerk-esque synths and rich guitars to create a style that presaged Depeche Mode and the Cure. To an outsize degree, the Swiss scene was recognized in turn by the British. John Peel promoted Mittageisen, and the fashion designer (herself Swiss, but affiliated with the British icon Vivian Westwood) Julia Seemann designed a collection in tribute to the band in 2016.

Mittageisen were still a part of the national Swiss, and broader German-language, scene. They collaborated with Grauzone member Marco Repetto and worked with German producers. Distinctive of the Swiss scene, they also had a female member, Ursula Sommerhalder. The most Swiss thing about the band is indeed their connection to Britain, both as a commercial market and as a source of genuine artistic inspiration. The multilingual, neutral culture of Switzerland perhaps predisposed its bands to engage in genuine international exchange. Or maybe it was just chance that John Peel and other British tastemakers adopted the scene. Nonetheless, Swiss groups like Grauzone, Liliput, and Mittageisen complicate our understanding of how international listeners engaged with neue deutsche Welle.

Race and Neue Deutsche Welle

The Austrians and the Swiss are not the only "others" of the neue deutsche Welle scene. The Germans' neighbors provide points of significant, yet not genre-defying, comparison. There is another, internal other that is itself defined and (mis)characterized by neue deutsche Welle artists themselves. This other is the racialized one. Neue deutsche Welle was generally a progressive genre. However, its portrayal of nonwhite people and non-European cultures could verge from insensitive to downright racist.

First, there is the presence of orientalism in neue deutsche Welle. Popularized by the academic Edward Said, orientalism refers to the stereotypical cultural representation of a vaguely construed "East" (typically Asia, the Middle East, or North Africa) as simultaneously exotic and alluring, and foreign and threatening. Many NDW artists released songs that played on the "Arabian Nights" trope, for example, 1. Futurologischer Congress' "Lawrence of Arabia," Mittlere Katastrophen Kapelle's "Arabische Nächte" ("Arabian Nights"), and Falco's "Nothin' Sweeter than Arabia." United Ball's 1981 hit "Pogo in Togo" exhibits a similar exotification, here directed at African countries. A more classical type of orientalism, sometimes couched in a poorly articulated critique of Islam, is exhibited in Cora's "Istanbul," DÖF's "Arafat," Korpus Kristi's "Tai," and again by Falco in both "Tut-Ench-Amom (Tutankhamun)" and "Die Königin von Eschnapur" ("The Queen of Eschnapur"). In these songs, Arab, Middle Eastern, and Asian countries are used as foreign set-dressing to create an exotic mood.

A different sort of neo orientalism is present in neue deutsche Welle with regard to Japan. For example, Andreas

Dorau's "Taxi nach Shibuya" ("Taxi to Shibuya"), Andy Giorbino's "Modernes Japan" ("Modern Japan"), and Eiskalte Engel's "Fudjiyama" all ostensibly portray Japan as an enviable modern to which West Germany can aspire. This comparison is not unwarranted; after all, both countries were Axis Powers during the Second World War that had to rebuild during the postwar era and consequently went through respective "economic miracles." However, these songs are not engaging in considered retellings of postwar economic development. More often they are reproducing exoticized motifs with synth instrumentation or delivering gibberish, Japanese-sounding nonsense lyrics. This only feeds into racist stereotypes, rather than furthering genuine trans-regional comparison.

Despite the considerable presence of people of Asian descent (especially Vietnamese immigrants) in Germany, there are vanishingly few examples of Asian artists in neue deutsche Welle. The most prominent examples are Young Hack Chi, who was a member of the bands Hamburger Arroganz, Partner Eins, and die Marinas (Andreas Dorau's backing band), Sid Gautama, the Indonesia-born drummer for several bands, including Bernward Büker Bande and Prima Klima; and Marc Chung, who was at times a member of Abwärts and Einstürzende Neubauten, among other groups.

Indigenous peoples are also misrepresented in neue deutsche Welle. Take, for example, the band Asphaltindianer ("Asphalt Indians") and their self-titled, 1982 EP. Nena have a song entitled "Indianer" ("Indians"), in which the subject and her partner claim to be strong, smart Indians, on the "warpath," living in their "wigwam." Most of the song's vocal track is comprised of stereotypical "war cries." Xmal

Deutschland's 1981 B-side "Großstadtindianer" ("Big-City Indians") also employs this racist sound effect, playing with the concept of "cowboys and Indians." Even Liliput, for all their progressive treatment of gender politics and experimental sound, have a song entitled "Wig Wam." The minor group Erste weibliche Fleischergesellin nach 1945 are most notable for using racist caricatures of Native Americans as a part of their releases. The band's biggest single was "Winnetou und Die 7 Geißlein" ("Winnetou and the Seven Kid Goats," 1982); its cover features a childlike, heavily stereotyped drawing of a shirtless "noble savage," perched on a cliff, overlooking rock formations that evoke the American southwest. The album likewise features toy figurines of war-bonnet-wearing Indians in a canoe or seated by a tipi. The titular "Winnetou" is a fictional creation of the German novelist Karl May, who wrote in the late 1800s. Winnetou is ostensibly an Indigenous person of the Great Plains, but everything about his character, from his mystical relationship with nature to his reverence for the warrior lifestyle, exemplifies the racist noble savage stereotype. Unfortunately, the appearance of these harmful tropes comes as no surprise; these neue deutsche Welle songs are examples of a broader trend in (both East and West) German popular culture. May's novels gave rise not only to a character but to an entire movement referred to by the academic Hartmut Lutz as "Indianthusiasm." This phenomenon consists of German people developing an affinity for Indigenous peoples—an affinity that is often one-sided, based in stereotype, and appropriative. Indianthusiasm manifested most directly in the collection of ephemera and the cosplaying of Indians by Germans at large gatherings.[17] Essentially, this phenomenon operates something like the usage of Native American caricatures as mascots or costumes, only on a larger, pseudo-communal scale.

Finally, neue deutsche Welle artists also exhibited anti-Black racism. Black people are used as pseudo-progressive props in the music video for Edelweiss' "Bring Me Edelweiss," which depicts several Black women and men in Austrian folk dress. It is possible that the women are background singers on the track, or they may be lip-synching—it is difficult to tell from the credits. The men may be the credited rappers Raf and Cooly C, though that too is unclear. None of these performers appeared as a part of the band in their 1989 Top of the Pops appearance. While asserting the possibility that people of color can have a claim to the Austrian identity via folk costume is a political statement, given that this music video also makes use of little people as a visual gag, it is hard to read that level of considered intent into the choice.

Worryingly common was the predisposition of neue deutsche Welle artists to use the "n-word" in their music. The band FEE does so in their song "Amerika," as does 1. Futurologischer Congress in their 1982 song "Rote Autos" ("Red Cars"). Both of these songs are ostensibly critiques of racism and police violence in the United States; however, that by no means makes it appropriate for white German artists to use a slur for Black African Americans. Other songs drop all

[17] See Hartmut Lutz, Florentine Strzelczyk, and Renae Watchman (eds.), *Indianthusiasm: Indigenous Responses* (Waterloo: Wilfrid Laurier University Press, 2020).

pretense of critiquing racism, for example, Andreas Dorau's song "N***rmuskeln" ("N****r muscles"), released as a B-side in 1981, which objectifies the bodies of Black men, and Joachim Witt's 1982 song "Ich bin der deutsche N***r ("I am the German N****r"), in which Witt seems to compare the social rejection he faces, potentially from women or nebulous authority figures, to the plight of Black people in the United States. This kind of equivalency is not unheard of in post-punk and new wave music, which sometimes traded on appropriation to a fault, exhibiting cultural amnesia toward historical and ongoing cultures of racism. Mark E. Smith of the seminal English post-punk group the Fall used the "n-word" to such effect in his song "The Classical." Whether its usage in NDW stems from homegrown German racism or the influence of British musicians, it is an unacceptable stain on the reputation of neue deutsche Welle.

6 The Turn to Tanz, Deutschrap, and Neue Deutsche Welle Revival

The Cold War was the defining political context of neue deutsche Welle; its end also spelled the end of the genre. On the evening of November 9, 1989, the East German Communist Party official Günter Schabowski gave a press conference in which he announced that all citizens of the German Democratic Republic would be allowed to apply to travel, or even emigrate permanently, to the West, effectively reopening all border crossings between the German Democratic Republic and West Germany. This sudden reversal of policy had not been the original intent of the East German government. Somewhere along the chain of command, the message got muddled and Schabowski, who had no hand in setting the new policy, ended up communicating a change that was far more liberal than anyone anticipated. Immediately, people began streaming through border crossings, traveling from East to West Berlin. Border guards, as confused about the sudden change in policy as the party apparatus, let them go peacefully. The Berlin Wall did not "fall" in 1989—it was opened.

A fortuitously timed *NME* article captures the opening of the Berlin Wall as experienced by the neue deutsche Welle community. It follows a group of former NDW musicians (from Palais Schaumburg and Ideal), who now play electronic music (dubbed "neue deutsche Tanz"), as they attend what they call "the biggest rave this century," the night the wall came down.[1] These musicians were aware that they were experiencing an important historical event and that their changed cultural output would come to be a defining feature of the turn. Berlin's new wave and rave cultures are linked. There is a continuity not only of musicians but also of attitude and public performance. The beats changed, but the people making them, the partygoers dancing to them, and the political atmosphere that bound the whole scene together did not. The list of neue deutsche Welle artists who went on to make dance music is endless. Sometimes, these artists or bands kept their stage names but shifted the genre of their output. Other times, they formed new bands or renamed their projects. 1. Futurologischer Congress, for example, continued to make music into the 1990s, and even had a few releases in the 2010s, though their output changed to incorporate more trance and rap influences. Falco is another artist whose music became more "computerized" and club-friendly in the late 1980s, and he too is the blueprint for the incorporation of hip-hop stylings into neue deutsche Welle.

Antecedents to the 1990s dance-pop movement also appear in neue deutsche Welle. Take, for example, bubblegum hits like Ixi's "Der Knutschfleck" ("The Lipstick Stain") or Paso

---

[1] Jack Barron, "Breaks for the Border," *New Musical Express*, November 25, 1989.

Doble's "Herz an Herz" ("Heart to Heart"). This strain of sugary, radio-friendly dance NDW was eagerly adopted by the dance scene. "Herz an Herz" was covered, in full Eurodance style, by the singer and model Blümchen in 1995. In their 1996 single "Wenn er vor mir steht" ("When He Stands before Me"), Eurodance trio die Kranken Schwestern reference "Ich will Spaß" through a lyrical interpolation. The continued influence of NDW into the 1990s worked through the persistent occupation of many of its musicians in creative industries and references to or reworkings of the genre's hits by new artists.

This continued cultural capital of neue deutsche Welle can be attributed in large part to the ongoing relevancy of the Cold War, even after the opening of the Berlin Wall. In these early, post-Cold-War years, the development of a phenomenon that would later come to be known as *Ostalgie*, or nostalgia for the East, emerged. *Ostalgie* is a complicated concept. It encourages the romanticization of life under a repressive regime, sometimes to the detriment of very real histories of oppression and subjugation. Simultaneously, it is important to challenge existing narratives of the Cold War that paint the West as a land of unequivocal freedom and the East as a totalitarian hellscape. People lived full lives in East Germany. They socialized, made music, and danced. Even post-1989, the historian Frederick Taylor asserts that East Berlin still has a reputation for being "more interesting" than the "sedate and sanitized" West. It has more clubs, experimental theaters, and cultural venues.[2] Though the wall is long gone, its political

[2] Frederick Taylor, *The Berlin Wall: A World Divided, 1961-1989* (New York: HarperCollins, 2006), 448.

memory is kept alive because it fuels Berlin's cultural output. Today, the former East Berlin has become something of an artists' haven: a cheaper area to live in that attracts young people, immigrants, and low-income creatives. Unfortunately, many of these same neighborhoods are also experiencing speculative real estate practices, gentrification, and rapidly rising rents. One must ask whether the thriving cultural scene of East Berlin can survive in a capitalist economy.

This question is of even greater importance to the marginalized people for whom nightlife was a refuge, namely, the members of the LGBTQ community who use the club as a site for community-building. This practice persists post-reunification, exemplified by the superclub Berghain. Berghain began as Ostgut, a club "known for its gay/straight mix and Saturday night techno parties that drew a liberated, body-conscious crowd." Opened in 1998, it closed in 2003 and was reborn as Berghain.[3] Described as "so stereotypically underground Berlin in every way, it could have been invented by a parodist," Berghain "emerged from a gay male S/M scene" and is "housed in a vast industrial building," a former heating plant.[4] It is notorious for its image-based, capricious door policy, which often leaves admission up to the sole discretion of its longtime bouncer, Sven Marquardt. In 2016, the club received a special designation for cultural venues, which allows it to pay a lower tax rate. More than just a club, one journalist remarked that Berghain is home to the same "anarchic energies set free

---

[3] Sunshine Flint, "The Club Scene, on the Edge," *New York Times*, December 12, 2004, TR4.
[4] Russell Smith, "Berghain and the Cult of Exclusivity," *Toronto: The Globe and Mail*, August 22, 2014, L2.

by [the fall of the wall]."[5] The political energy born of NDW lives on in the club culture of today.

The legacies of neue deutsche Welle live on into the twenty-first century. Today, NDW influences can be found in Deutschrap, German rap music. Deutschrap and neue deutsche Welle are not dissimilar. Both genres began in the 1980s and were inspired by foreign, English-speaking scenes— in the case of NDW, Britain and for Deutschrap, America. While neue deutsche Welle gained popularity quickly before fading away, Deutschrap has grown steadily over time. Its trajectory has mirrored the mainstream popularization of rap music in the United States. While, in the 1980s and 1990s, the genre was seen as marginal and even dangerous (largely because of its racialization), by the 2010s rap had become part of the mainstream. This popularization brings with it discourses of authenticity, though these will not be the focus of this section.

While the primary influence of Deutschrap is hip-hop and rap as originated by African Americans in the United States, Deutschrap is, chronologically, the next identifiably German genre of music to come after neue deutsche Welle. As many Deutschrappers seek to make the genre more identifiably German, it is not uncommon for them to turn to neue deutsche Welle as a source of cultural symbols, which they recontextualize within their specific experiences, as financially disadvantaged people (often "Ossis"— residents of former East Germany), (the children of) immigrants, or other racialized minorities in Germany.

---

[5] John Pareles, "Still Partying in the Ruins," *New York Times*, November 23, 2014, TR1.

For example, the rap duo SXTN's 2016 song "Ich bin Schwarz" ("I Am Black") interpolates the melody from Markus' "Ich will Spaß." Both songs discuss wanting to have a good time as a young German person. In a lighthearted tone, rappers Nura and Juju discuss driving while Black in Germany and the increased police attention that they garner as racialized women. They attempt to reclaim racist stereotypes, proclaiming that they are loud, sell weed, have a natural affinity for music, and love twerking. They make fun of (presumably white) Germans who try to touch their hair and boast that they too have German passports now. SXTN's song is provocative, revealing a deeper truth about racism in German society: the reckless, antisocial behavior of white German youths is far more likely to be excused and overlooked (and to top charts as a lighthearted party song) than that same behavior is when exhibited by young Germans of color. This comparison is underscored through the use of a classic neue deutsche Welle song, a recognizable cultural touchstone of the now-older German generation.

Falco in particular has added relevance here. Not only was he one of the biggest stars of neue deutsche Welle, he was also the first Deutschrapper, although he was not identified as such at the time. It follows, then, that his music is referenced many times over by practitioners of the genre today. For example, on the song "NDW 2005" off his album *Neue Deutsche Welle*, the rapper Fler samples "Rock Me Amadeus," declaring Deutschrap to be the new neue deutsche Welle, in protest against American pop music. Worryingly, on this album, Fler was criticized for using nationalist speech and aesthetics under the guise of being a "proud German." German nationalism, especially when combined with bravado and performative violence, becomes evocative of fascistic rhetoric.[6] It is almost ironic that this kind of controversy would surround an album that samples Falco, who is a Deutschrapper only insofar as he raps in the German language. In all other respects, he represents a distinct Austrian identity, a concept that poses a challenge to pan-German nationalism.

Other artists have used Falco's music to more progressive ends. The 2018 album *Sterben um zu Leben* (*"Dying to Live"*) presents twelve Falco tracks, remixed and featuring different Deutschrappers, including artists of Afsharid Cuban, and Pakistani descent. While many of the songs discuss the legacy of Falco as a Deutschrapper, or compare Falco's own hard-partying, cocaine-dependent lifestyle to the indulgences of present-day musicians, some of the rappers address the role of their marginal identities in their music. For example, on his remix of "Rock Me Amadeus," the Ukrainian-Jewish rapper Sun Diego, who immigrated to Germany as a child, declares his Jewish identity and implies that it is significant that "a Jew is now making neue deutsche Welle." This statement subverts the traditional notion of who has access to the German identity—all the more so because of the omnipresent history of the Holocaust. Sun Diego presents a more optimistic vision of German identity, in which a Jewish artist can become the torchbearer of a quintessentially German cultural artifact such as neue deutsche Welle. Sun Diego follows the example of Falco, placing himself in the

---

[6] Uh-Young Kim, "Skandal-Rap: Fler und Er," *Spiegel*, May 23, 2005, https://www.spiegel.de/kultur/musik/skandal-rap-fler-und-er-a-356560.html.

artistic legacy of musical genius that runs from Mozart, to Falco, and now to the Deutschrappers of today, no matter where their families come from or whether they are ethnically German.

Deutschrappers also invoke the legacy of 1990s dance music in their neue deutsche Welle references. For example, on his 2021 song "Herzalarm," the EDM-influenced Deutschrapper FiNCH collaborated with the 1990s trance-pop artist Blümchen, referencing many of her hits in the lyrics of the song, including her aforementioned cover of "Herz an Herz," as well as her rendition of Nena's "Nur geträumt." FiNCH creates a continuum of German musical culture that spans from the 1980s to the 2020s.

Not all crossovers between Deutschrap and neue deutsche Welle are amicable. The 2020 song "Hoes Up G's Down" by Shirin David exemplifies the dual influence of American rap and neue deutsche Welle on Deutschrap. The beat from the song is a sample from Jay-Z's 1997 song "(Always Be My) Sunshine" featuring Foxy Brown. Jay-Z's beat interpolates Kraftwerk's 1978 song "Die Mensch-Maschine" ("The Man-Machine"), by way of the Fearless Four's 1982 song "Rockin' It." David's lyrics point toward her American influences, referencing figures from hip-hop history, such as Tupac and Lil' Kim, while discussing how she finds feminine performance and consumerism empowering. The use of a beat by Kraftwerk (who were inspired by R&B, soul, and Motown music, and in turn inspired some early hip-hop[7]), filtered through the lens

[7] John Morrison, "Kraftwerk and Black America: A Musical Dialogue," *The Wire*, May 2020, https://www.thewire.co.uk/in-writing/essays/kraftwerk-john-morrison.

of Jay-Z, makes the sonic messaging of "Hoes Up G's Down" sophisticated. This sample gestures at a broader history of the international, circular exchange between English- and German-speaking cultural producers. However, Kraftwerk member Ralf Hütter did not take kindly to David's use of the interpolated sample and took legal action. In 2023, a new version of the song with a different beat was released. The official reason for the lawsuit was that the sample was used without the permission of Hütter, who did not want "Shirin David to drive a jetski in a pool to the tune of his beat" (as she does in the music video).[8] This particular intergenerational, inter-genre relationship remains fraught.

Nonetheless, Deutschrap presents the most compelling successor to neue deutsche Welle. It is distinctively German in a way that neue deutsche Tanz, which had broad connections to the Eurodance scene, was not and seeks not only to cash out on the symbols of NDW but to subvert them to formulate new, more inclusive understandings of German identity. Deutschrappers, like neue deutsche Welle musicians before them, have returned to the well of English-language culture and, while their appropriation of an inherently Black cultural form is problematic in the same way that post punk and new wave's usage of the sonic motifs of dub music was, there is at least a more conscious effort to diversify Germany identity and push back against racism (as well as classism and sexism) domestically.

---

[8]"Shirin David: Zoff mit Kraftwerk wegen Sample," *Laut*, January 11, 2023, https://www.laut.de/News/Shirin-David-Zoff-mit-Kraftwerk-wegen-Sample--11-01-2023-19363.

Contemporaneously, a more literal revival of post-punk and new wave is under way in Germany. This revival is responsible for a broader renewed interest in neue deutsche Welle, which occasionally does occur in tandem with the recontextualization of NDW motifs in Deutschrap. For example, at the 2019 Red Bull Music Clash, a festival-like event sponsored by the energy drink manufacturer, which has an established history of supporting both electronic dance music and now rap in Germany, the Deutschrapper Bausa engaged in a song battle against the mainstream pop artist Lena (who represented Germany at Eurovision in 2010 and 2011). The artists were challenged to reinterpret Nena's "99 Luftballons." Lena's version is a more traditional rendering, largely keeping the song as is, but updating the instrumentation and interpolating Jay-Z's "99 Problems," a similar attempt to tie neue deutsche Welle to American hip-hop culture via Deutschrap. Bausa's cover, on the other hand, rewrites the lyrics of the original song. Titled "99 Schuhkartons" ("99 Shoeboxes"), the cover is about sneakerhead culture. Bausa's cover is true to Nena's original in that he sings, rather than raps, the song, preserving its melody. Neue deutsche Welle revival therefore brings Deutschrappers into the pop-rock mainstream.

German-speaking indie bands also constitute the neue deutsche Welle revival. In the early 2000s, beginning with the Strokes and then growing to include bands like the Killers, the Arctic Monkeys, and Franz Ferdinand, post-punk revival emerged as a major trend in the independent, or "indie," music scene in the United States and Great Britain. These post-punk revival bands did not reproduce the exact sounds of the 1970s and 1980s, avoiding kitschy overuse of synthesizer and drum machines while still wearing their influences on their sleeve. Melodic guitar and bass lines, sensitive-voiced lead singers, and crisp, danceable drum beats abound in English-language, post-punk revival music. While there was no German-language equivalent to the post-punk revival at this time (although many of these American and British bands were and remain popular in German-speaking markets), one would follow later.

The best example of the German-language post-punk revival, which could be dubbed "neue deutsche Welle revival," is the Austrian band Bilderbuch. Formed in 2008, Bilderbuch are an indie band (since 2015 all their music has been self-released on Maschin Records); however, their music incorporates a wide variety of influences. Not only do they use the melodic guitar of post-punk and new wave music, their production is influenced by electronic music, and their lyrical delivery takes cues from hip-hop. This is a mixing of different historical German music genres: neue deutsche Welle, neue deutsche Tanz, and Deutschrap. Bilderbuch, as an Austrian group, are also operating in the specific legacy of Falco. His influence is apparent in the blending of avant-garde pop forms with the lyrical cadence of hip-hop which, in the German-language context, can be attributed to him.

Many of the larger themes addressed by Bilderbuch are ones that Falco devoted attention to: cultural capital, class, and social hierarchy. In songs like "Schick Schock," "Kitsch," and "OM," Bilderbuch poke fun at financial inequality and garish displays of material wealth, the simultaneous sophisticated shame and naive joy of indulging in kitsch, and the commodification of new-age ideas of wellness by self-styled Western health gurus. Their music is a critique of twenty-first-century culture and society. Grappling with new technologies and ideas in an increasingly globalized world is a core theme of new wave music on the whole, neue deutsche Welle specifically, and Falco personally.

The revival of post-punk and new wave forms in the German-speaking world is not defined by the activities and outputs of individual artists. Neither, in the age of the internet, is it domestically bounded. Today, Germany is a center of internationally minded post-punk and new wave artists. It is an important stopover for many new wave revival bands from the Soviet Union. Notably, the Belarusian post-punk trio Molchat Doma, whose second album was picked up by the Berlin-based Detriti Records, after their first, self-released effort was discovered online. The band eventually signed with the New York label Sacred Bones. Molchat Doma, whose music is performed in Russian, have toured Europe (especially Germany) many times and have in recent years undertaken world tours of the United States, Latin America, and even Australia. The German market provides an important gateway for bands from all around the world to break into the global market. It might be a radical reimagining of the neue deutsche Welle genre to call bands that do not sing in German and are not of German origin NDW, but that worldwide cultural network as displayed by post-punk and new wave revival is indicative of the global potential of the genre, which went unrealized by its biggest stars of the 1980s.

Artists outside of Germany also sing in the German language in homage to the genre. For example, on her 2020 self-titled album, the American new wave revival artist Riki performed several songs in German, including "Strohmann" ("Strawman") and "Böse Lügen" ("Evil Lies"). For revival artists the use of German becomes a cultural symbol in the same way that English was for first-generation neue deutsche Welle musicians. Singing in German allows Riki to reference the long history of NDW artists and put her work in the context of their historical lineage. This positioning reveals that forty years after the highpoint of the genre, NDW still has cultural capital and is a desirable point of reference, connoting 1980s Cold War retromania and the coolness of the Berlin club scene. Some domestic German bands working in this mode include Nils Keppel, Steintor Herrenchor, and Temmis, which were all dubbed "Neue Neue Deutsche Welle" by the German-language music publication *DIFFUS*.[9]

Finally, neue deutsche Welle revival exists outside the musical realm, in music and television. One early example is the 2003 film *Verschwende deine Jugend* ("*Waste Your Youth*"), directed by Benjamin Quabeck, which follows a young bank clerk who dreams of seeing DAF live in concert. The film's soundtrack features many songs by neue deutsche Welle and British new wave bands alike. A similar, more contemporary example is the soundtrack of the 2017 American action film *Atomic Blond*, which is set in Cold War Berlin. It featured "Major Tom (Völlig losgelöst)," "99 Luftballons" (both the original and a cover by English-German post-punk revival band Kaleida), and "Der Kommissar." The film engages in a stylized, hauntological

---

[9] Pia Schneider, "NNDW-Sounds aus der Pfalz: Nils Keppel veröffentlicht '222,'" *DIFFUS*, https://diffusmag.de/p/nndw-sounds-aus-der-pfalz-nils-keppel-veroeffentlicht-222/#.

romanticization of the Cold War, a pattern that can be observed in German media as well, namely the *Deutschland 83/86/89* television series (each run of the three-season show is named after the year in which it is set), released between 2015 and 2020. The show references neue deutsche Welle both diegetically and in its soundtrack. The version of the opening titles produced for the British and American markets uses the English-language version of "Major Tom (Völlig losgelöst)" (the German version uses New Order's "Blue Monday"), the script references Falco as the "biggest German-speaking popstar," the show was scored by the prominent neue deutsche Welle musician and producer Reinhold Heil, who worked with both Nena and Nina Hagen, and the soundtrack features countless neue deutsche Welle hits.[10] Finally, a television remake of the film *Christiane F.*, titled *Wir Kinder vom Bahnhof Zoo*, was released in 2021. Targeted to a teenage audience, this series brought the neue deutsche Welle canon into the age of streaming, for a new generation. Through nostalgic (and *ostalgisch*) revival, the subculture and the microtrend have become one.

---

[10]Florian Cossen (dir.), "Tar Baby," *Deutschland 86*, Amazon Prime, October 19, 2018.

Conclusion: Dualities of Geopolitics and Genre

The high point of neue deutsche Welle was 1981 to 1984, but the genre has both a longer history and an ongoing legacy. The NDW "moment" is a rich historical text, a time when cultural production occurred so fast that boom and bust trend cycles happened nearly simultaneously, but this conceptualization is reductive. Neue deutsche Welle has both the trappings of a larger, subcultural movement and a flash-in-the-pan microtrend. Its practitioners took inspiration from punk, post-punk, and new wave subgenres in order to create a rich and varied sound that is impossible to categorize as underground or commercial (not unlike the hyperpop music of the 2020s). While this experimentation was reviled by some hardcore rock and punk fans, neue deutsche Welle was largely considered to be an innovative, experimental scene with the potential to adapt English-language cultural markers to not only the language but also the specific sociopolitical context of West Germany, Austria, and Switzerland.

Much early neue deutsche Welle music is best described as avant-garde, both for its ties to the art scene and because experimentation with electronic instrumentation, industrial sounds, and the usage of silence (influenced by dub) were all important features of independent neue deutsche Welle music. Many of these features were borrowed from the British and American scenes, but they also connected to the distinct experiences of postwar German youth. Broader postwar trends in economic development and urban decline manifested in Germany, but the unique media market and near-complete political monoculture of the Federal Republic of Germany were defining features of the postwar West German experience. Especially for young people, the independent NDW scene provided an alternative, more representative cultural mode. In Berlin, Hamburg, and Düsseldorf, the scene was strong enough not just to support a few local bands but to create a broader network of creatives, media institutions, and cultural producers. NDW communities became self-sustaining alternative spaces that provided ways for disaffected people to make a living without subjecting themselves to mainstream conformity. These disaffected groups included women (although NDW also reproduced societal misogyny) and LGBTQ people.

The Cold War context was also crucial to neue deutsche Welle. At the time, Germany was in fact two countries, and there was no immediate vision of a reunified future. The Federal Republic of Germany and the German Democratic Republic developed independent cultural scenes, which nonetheless shared a history and engaged in cross-pollination based on geographic proximity and a shared language. Neue deutsche Welle is no exception; though the genre originated in West Germany, East German cultural producers (i.e., the state) were aware of the movement and supported it. The East German government would come to create their own neue deutsche Welle artists, who operated in the aesthetic mode of mainstream, commercial NDW musicians from the West, despite the fact that the East German cultural production machine worked according to state dictum, not the forces of market capitalism. The Cold War was also a prominent theme in neue deutsche Welle music. Many of the genre's most famous hits are about the Cold War in some fashion. They express frustration with the positionality of West Germany as a country in the middle of the conflict, beholden to its American ally, split by the Iron Curtain, and unable to make decisions free from overpowering US and Soviet influences. The threat of war, whether fought with nuclear warheads or rocket ships, hung over only newly rebuilt Germany and manifested in its music.

These political themes demonstrate the close relationship between the avant-garde, underground and the mainstream, commercial strands of neue deutsche Welle. The pop side of NDW did not eschew political themes for the sake of finding the broadest possible audience. Many of the genre's biggest hits are political songs. Likewise, plenty of songs from the underground only gesture at punk notions of "no future" or youth discontent, while remaining derivative and politically inert. Worse is when these supposedly subversive artists blame women for their problems. Just as plenty of independent artists lacked true political consciousness, many mainstream neue deutsche Welle musicians were politically aware. This observation does not degenerate the underground or valorize the mainstream. It reveals the fact that the "divided" neue deutsche Welle scene was more coherent than popular narratives portray. This is also reinforced by the career trajectories of many NDW artists. It was not uncommon for musicians to change styles, be involved in more than one project, or work in multiple roles within the industry. Many artists maintained simultaneous connections to both the independent and commercial scenes, organically moving back and forth between the two "sides" of NDW without penalty to their careers.

The divisions between the West German neue deutsche Welle scene and other national scenes were more "real." While East German NDW was formally cordoned off from the rest of the genre's practitioners, neue deutsche Welle musicians in Austria and Switzerland had more contact with their German co-creatives. The shared German language made for a natural point of commonality between these three scenes, but the Austrians and the Swiss retained their individuality. The Swiss scene, despite being small, achieved a high degree of renown not only among German-speaking audiences but also in the UK. Swiss artists were not distinct from German ones because they incorporated any kind of recognizable Swiss cultural symbolism into their music. Rather, they stood out because their scene became an object of interest for British post-punk and new wave aficionados. The international new wave did not simply travel from Britain and break upon (metaphorical) German, Swiss, and Austrian shores. It rebounded, creating a current of cultural exchange and ongoing communication between continental Europe and the UK. The Austrian artist Falco was equally distinct. His music was unabashedly Austrian; he sang in a strong Viennese dialect and referenced both the contemporary politics of his country and its centuries-long imperial history under the Habsburg dynasty. Nonetheless,

Falco's crossover appeal and clever incorporation of pop stylings into the spirit of the independent underground are quintessentially neue deutsche Welle. He is proof that NDW is only German in the linguistic sense; it is not bound by political borders or nationality.

NDW was still an exclusionary genre, at times. Despite its progressive trappings, the neue deutsche Welle scene replicated racist tropes. Orientalism was common. Reprehensible German attitudes toward Indigenous peoples were also found in neue deutsche Welle songs. Anti-Black racism was common too. This prejudice was the most insidious, because it worked on several levels. The "n-word" can be found in a number of NDW songs; Black people and the racism they face were used for rhetorical shock value. Simultaneously, the neue deutsche Welle sound, like post-punk music in general, was derived from dub, a type of music that grew out of reggae and was pioneered by Black people. Globally, new wave, including neue deutsche Welle, was dominated by white people with little consideration of this history.

Neue deutsche Welle did not radically change until 1989 and the effective end of the Cold War in both Germanys, which reunified into one country. Neue deutsche Welle, which had been so tied to the Cold War, could not survive in the postwar era, but neither was it destroyed. It evolved—largely through its artists, who moved on to different instruments, techniques, and musical projects. Still, neue deutsche Tanz was not as unique to the German-language context as NDW had been; it was part of a larger Eurodance movement. However, the next distinguishably German genre to emerge, Deutschrap, would be directly influenced by neue deutsche Welle. The afterlives of neue deutsche Welle in Deutschrap go beyond sampling culture or superficial reference. They show a concentrated effort to build a unique cultural lineage, once more rooted in language, rather than nationality. Indeed, there are many German and Swiss Deutschrappers, as well as some Austrians. Even more important than the political citizenship of these artists are their diverse backgrounds, which demonstrate the multiethnic nature of the contemporary German national project (even as many Deutschrappers criticize said project). NDW has also gone through a more literal revival, akin to the early 2000s post-punk revival that occurred in Britain and the United States.

It is tempting to view the reemergence of neue deutsche Welle as a form of retromania or cultural recycling—the cheap use of nostalgia in order to induce emotionally driven consumption.[1] This straightforward narrative of the commercial appropriation of the subculture does not describe the full complexity of this cultural cycle. It is more accurate to say that the reappearance of the forms and symbols of neue deutsche Welle in the cultural consciousness represents a reexamination and refashioning of German history and identity on a number of levels. First, it signifies a reckoning with the Cold War, insofar as neue deutsche Welle is a hallmark of late-Cold War cultural anxieties. As historians seek to diversify the narratives of the Cold War and show that the conflict was not so dichotomous, divided Germany becomes a productive subject for historical analysis. Neue deutsche Welle music's incisive view of the Cold

---

[1] As coined in Simon Reynolds, *Retromania: Pop Culture's Addiction to Its Own Past* (New York: Farrar, Straus, and Giroux, 2011).

War and the fraught position that West Germany found itself in has only become more relevant as these complex narratives have gained greater significance.

The reconsideration of neue deutsche Welle in light of the advent of Deutschrap is also significant. It represents an effort by first- or second-generation Germans to lay claim to a cultural legacy that many would deny them on the basis of xenophobia. The ability of Germany to handle large inflows of migrants, as professed in 2015 by then chancellor Angela Merkel, has proven to be one of the most pressing political questions of the twenty-first century thus far, and Deutschrap's own interpolation of neue deutsche Welle melodies, symbols, and themes is just one avenue by which these new artists are asserting their right to participate in a historic German identity while also shaping said identity to include their unique experiences. In doing so, they are also correcting the historical racisms of the 1980s neue deutsche Welle scene, reclaiming the progressive elements of the genre and not allowing its contributions to German culture to be undercut by the insensitivities of some of its practitioners.

Reexamining neue deutsche Welle allows for a reconceptualization of the relationship between authenticity and commerciality. The tension between these two factors is perennial to artistic production. Comfortingly, the study of neue deutsche Welle shows that an aesthetic sensibility, whether it be visual or auditory, does not have any fixed or inherent political connotations. Even once certain aesthetic symbols are imbued with political significance, they can always be de- or re-politicized. This phenomenon is demonstrated by the spectrum of artists that created music under the banner of neue deutsche Welle: politically charged pop music, highly derivative underground noise, empty chart fodder, and avant-garde sonic experiments all can be located within the auditory boundaries of neue deutsche Welle. An artist who created a teeny-bopper bubblegum hit one year could be found making industrial noise on an independent record label the next, and vice versa. Many musicians made such migrations several times over or coexisted in both the commercial and underground sectors of the genre. It is never artistically productive to pit "real" musicians against "sell-outs." Neue deutsche Welle is proof of that; the genre transcends the West German postwar experience to offer broader lessons that should shape our attitude toward cultural production and consumption into the twenty-first century and beyond.

10 Essential Tracks

1. **Einstürzende Neubauten, "Steh auf Berlin,"** *Kollaps* **(Hamburg, FRG: ZickZack, ZZ 65, 1981).**

"Steh auf Berlin" ("I Love Berlin") is the second song off Einstürzende Neubauten's first studio album, *Kollaps*. Featuring band members Blixa Bargeld, F. M. Einheit (Frank Martin Strauß), and N. U. Unruh (Andrew Chudy), the song (and the album as a whole) is characterized by its industrial instrumentation and "no future" lyrics. The opening seconds of "Steh auf Berlin" are dominated by the harsh noise of a jackhammer, which gives way to the percussive sounds of metal being hit, explosion sound effects, and Bargeld's screams. The lyrics of the song proclaim Bargeld's love for "decay," "sickness," "intoxication," and other products of modern, urban decline. This makes "Steh auf Berlin" a prototypical example of the "no future" mentality as it manifested in the Berlin scene—as the means by which musicians took ownership of their beloved, precarious city, transforming it from a crumbling "hell" into a creative epicenter.

2. **Malaria!, "Geld—Money,"** *Emotion* **(Berlin, FRG: Moabit Musik 002, 1982).**

"Geld—Money," the first track off Malaria!'s first album, is sung entirely in German, despite its bilingual title. The sound of falling coins punctuates a throbbing, ominous synth-and-drum machine instrumental. The song's lyrics proclaim that "money rules the world;" it has become the new religion of the modern age. "Geld—Money" embodies both the avant-garde instrumentation and criticism of global capitalism that pervaded neue deutsche Welle. Malaria! is more generally significant for being entirely composed of women—at the time, its members were Gudrun Gut, Bettina Köster, Susanne Kuhnke, Christine Hahn, and Manon P. Duursma. The album also received releases in Belgium, Italy, and Japan but never in an English-speaking country.

3. Neonbabies, "Blaue Augen," *I Don't Want to Loose You* (self-released, 1980).

"Blaue Augen" ("Blue Eyes") was first released in March 1980 on a four-track EP by the band Neonbabies. The original version of this song features less professional vocals, a prominent saxophone part, and a slower tempo—that is, in comparison to the other version of "Blaue Augen" recorded by the band Ideal that same year, which is faster and swaps in keyboard and guitar parts for the saxophone (played by Reinhard Meermann). Slightly (though not markedly) more commercial, Ideal's version charted in West Germany, Austria, and Switzerland. However, it is not a cover per se. The song was written and performed by Annette Humpe, who was at the time a member of both Neonbabies and Ideal. The two versions' lyrics are nearly identical, describing a lover with striking blue eyes. "Blaue Augen" exemplifies the cross-pollination and shared networks between the underground and mainstream scenes in neue deutsche Welle. Neonbabies would go on to put "Blaue Augen" on their first, self-titled album (Berlin, FRG: Good Noise, VGSN 2005, 1981). Conny Cool performed Bass,

Anton "Toni" Nissl drums, Nikolaus Polak guitar, and Annette's sister Inga additional vocals on the original version of the track, while Klaus D. Müller produced the rerecording.

4. Nena, "99 Luftballons," *Nena* (FRG: CBS 25 264, 1983).

Arguably the most popular neue deutsche Welle song of all time, "99 Luftballons" ("99 Balloons") was an international hit; its original German version reached number two on the US Billboard Hot 100. Instrumentally, "99 Luftballons" is a fairly straightforward pop song with new wave influences, such as a danceable beat and upbeat synths. Its most unique musical feature is a repeated ska breakdown. Lyrically, the song also draws upon mass appeal but in a subversive fashion. Gabriele "Nena" Kerner (the front woman and namesake of the band, which also included Jörn Uwe Fahrenkrog-Petersen on keyboards, Carlo Karges on guitar, Jürgen Dehmel on bass, and Rolf Brendel on drums) narrates a somewhat abstracted version of the experience of being a civilian during the Cold War, knowing that at any moment, the pride, greed, or simple incompetence of the men in charge of superpower regimes could annihilate all of humanity. "99 Luftballons" is not popular because of its commercial sound (the song was composed by Fahrenkrog-Petersen and produced by Reinhold Heil and Manfred Praeker), but rather because of the relatability of its message. That message was rendered in the original German by Carlo Karges, though a somewhat less explicitly political English version, with lyrics by Kevin McAlea, followed. Nena's self-titled album never received a US release (though it has been rereleased and repressed across European markets many times), but Epic released the English version of the song as a single in the United States and Canada in 1983.

5.   Die Doraus und die Marinas, "Fred vom Jupiter," *Blumen Und Narzissen* (Düsseldorf, FRG: Ata Tak, WR 12, 1981).

Released by the then sixteen-year-old Andreas Dorau as a single off his first album, "Fred vom Jupiter" ("Fred from Jupiter") features a backing choir of tweens, the so-called Marinas: Dagmar Petersen (13), Claudia Flohr (13), Michelle Milewski (14), Christine Süßmilch (12), and Isabelle Spelly (11). The ages of the Marinas are stated outright on the packaging for the single release of "Fred vom Jupiter," whose cover art is likewise childish, featuring toy dolls and a picturesque rendering of a house. However, "Fred vom Jupiter" was released on the independent Ata Tak label, also home to der Plan and Deutsch Amerikanische Freundschaft. The song's seemingly straightforward story, about a charming alien named Fred who comes to Earth, is also undercut by its ending, in which Fred must leave to prevent the men of Earth from reacting to his alien superiority with violent jealousy. Superficially, "Fred vom Jupiter" may seem like a children's song, and Dorau himself a teen idol, but it is actually a sophisticated work of subversion that plays on the childlike to ironic, critical effect. Mute licensed the single for release in the UK.

6.   Deutsch Amerikanische Freundschaft, "Der Mussolini," *Alles Gut* (London: Virgin, V2202, 1981).

"Der Mussolini" is the second track off Deutsch Amerikanische Freundschaft's third album (their second on a British label, after their first record was released by Warning Records, a predecessor to Ata Tak), which was released simultaneously by Virgin in the UK, Germany, and other European territories (however, the song was released as a single only in Germany). Featuring a relentlessly danceable synth-drum machine line, heavily edited backing vocals, and provocative lyrics that implore the listener to do various dances, including "the Communism," "the Mussolini," "the Jesus Christ," and the "Adolf Hitler," the song is frenetic. Songwriters Gabi Delgado-López and Robert Görl juxtapose totalitarian ideologies and leaders with lyrics and a beat that command the listener to dance, implicitly comparing the mass movements of history to the moving masses on the dance floor. Besides its nightclub-friendly sound, the album art (for both "Der Mussolini" as a single and the album *Alles Gut*), which featured shirtless portraits of a sweaty Delgado-López and Görl, indicates Deutsch Amerikanische Freundschaft's congruity with and importance to 1980s gay culture.

7. Joachim Witt, "Goldener Reiter," *Silberblick* (FRG: WEA 58 231, 1980).

"Goldener Reiter" ("Golden Rider") is another example of the potential for depth in commercial neue deutsche Welle. Downtempo, as far as hits (the song charted at number two in West Germany) go, "Goldener Reiter" deals (inexpertly) with themes of mental health and social alienation in a city implied to be Berlin. Released on an international record label (which took advantage of the song's success post-facto, rereleasing it as a single in 1981), it nonetheless features post-punk-influenced amateur vocals and a jangly guitar line, although its backing vocals are more pop-inspired. The music video exhibits a similar duality: Witt's dance moves are jerky and Ian Curtis-esque, but he is contraposed with a trio of conventionally attractive women in objectifying nurses' costumes. Witt himself composed the song and performed the vocals, guitar, organ, and synthesizer, while Harald Gutowski played bass and Jaki Liebezeit drums. Harald Grosskopf provided additional synthesizer.

8. Falco, "Wiener Blut," *Wiener Blut* (Austria: GiG Records 222 147, 1988).

The lead, titular single off Falco's fifth studio album is an underappreciated gem in his discography. Coming late in the life span of neue deutsche Welle, "Wiener Blut" ("Viennese Blood") illustrates that the longevity of the genre is greater than commonly understood. While *Wiener Blut* was Falco's first album not to hit number one in Austria (it "only" made it to second place), it received a cooler critical reception than his earlier releases. On "Wiener Blut," Falco (the stage name of Johann "Hans" Hölzel, who on this release again worked with longtime songwriting and production collaborators Rob and Ferdi Bolland) again employs his classic tropes: classical music samples contraposed with earworm synths, catchy lyrics sung in the Viennese dialect, and references to centuries of Austrian history.

9. Grauzone, "Eisbär," *Swiss Wave the Album* (Zürich, Switzerland: Off Course Records, ASL-3301, 1980).

Originally appearing on a compilation record of Swiss new wave bands before its release as a discrete single (Off Course Records, ASL-24) the next year, "Eisbär" ("Polar Bear") exemplifies the international reach of avant-garde neue deutsche Welle. At the time of recording, Grauzone consisted of guitarist and vocalist Martin Eicher, drummer Marco Repetto, bassist Christian "GT" Trüssel, and saxophonist Claudine Chirac. The song, which alternated between moments of sparse cold wave, punctuated by noise, was produced by Urs Steiger. However, the band soon underwent several lineup changes, before breaking up in 1982, in spite of their newfound success (in both the German-speaking world and abroad, specifically in the UK). They had unsuccessfully resisted releasing "Eisbär" as a single, though they managed to keep an English-language version of the song (whose lyrics, in either language, describe a desire to be an emotionally impervious polar bear, cold in both a literal and metaphorical sense) from release until 1998, when it appeared on the retrospective compilation CD *Die Sunrise Tapes* (Off Course Records, BIAS 331 CD).

10. Fehlfarben, "Ein Jahr (es geht voran)," *Monarchie und Alltag* (FRG: Welt-Rekord, EMI Electrola 1C 064-46 150).

"Ein Jahr (es geht voran)" ("One Year (It Goes On)"), the eighth song off the first album by Düsseldorf-based band Fehlfarben, was ahead of its time in several respects. As an album, *Monarchie und Alltag* ("*Monarchy and Daily Life*") was a slow-burn, not charting until seven months after its release. "Ein Jahr (es geht voran)" was only issued as a single in 1982 (Welt-Rekord, EMI Electrola 1A 006-46580), once sales picked up, but the song has come to be considered a classic of neue deutsche Welle, to the point that it was reissued in 2009 (Bureau B BB35) to take advantage of the broader post-punk revival movement.

Certainly, the song was politically prescient as well, notable for its discussion of failed space technology projects and their entanglement with the military brinksmanship of the Cold War. Musically, "Ein Jahr (es geht voran)" is prototypical post-punk. At the time Fehlfarben's lineup consisted of bassist Michael Kemner, drummer Uwe Bauer, guitarist Thomas Schwebel, saxophonist Frank Fenstermacher, synthesizer players George Nicolaidis and Kurt Dahlke, and singer Peter Hein.

Bibliography

Andresen, Willi. "Vitesse: Schnelle Jungs und flinke
    Schulmädchen." *Sounds*. January 1979.
Bächer, Hanna. "The Experimental Life of Pyrolator." *Red Bull Music
    Academy*. April 26, 2019. https://daily.redbullmusicacademy
    .com/2019/04/pyrolator-interview.
Banks, Robin. "Clash at the Apocalypse Hotel." *ZigZag*. November,
    1981.
Barron, Jack. "Breaks for the Border." *New Musical Express*.
    November 25, 1989.
Behrendt, Ralf. "Gesclunacksentwicklungen und Schubladen."
    Leserbriefe. *Sounds*. May 1980.
Berna, Marianne. "Kleenex: Heisse Sounds aus dem
    Schwiizerland." *Sounds*. February 1979.
Bigalke, Eva. "SOUNDS—Die Reifeprüfung?" Leserbriefe. *Sounds*.
    November 1979, 4.
Bohn, Chris. "Einstürzende Neubauten: Let's Hear It for the
    Untergang Show." *New Musical Express*. February 5, 1983.
Bottà, Giacomo. *Deindustrialisation and Popular Music: Punk and
    "Post-Punk" in Manchester, Düsseldorf, Torino, and Tampere*.
    London: Rowman & Littlefield, 2020.
Brandstetter, Thomas. "Imagining Inorganic Life: Crystalline Aliens
    in Science and Fiction." In *Imagining Outer Space: European
    Astroculture in the Twentieth Century*. Edited by Alexander C. T.
    Geppert, 73–94. London: Palgrave Macmillan, 2012.
Braunsteiner, Ewald. "Apologie eines apolitischen Stils: Am Ende
    der Disco-Ära." *Sounds*. March 1980, 24–5.

Brock, Hella and Christoph Kleinschmidt (eds.). *Jugendlexikon: Musik*. Leipzig, Deutsche Demokratische Republik: VEB Bibliographisches Institut, 1983.

Buttler, Thomas. "Mit 'Njuhwehf' in die Eiszeit." SOUNDS Diskurs. *Sounds*. July 1980.

Cateforis, Theo. *Are We Not New Wave?: Modern Pop at the Turn of the 1980s*. Tracking Pop. Ann Arbor: University of Michigan Press, 2011.

Cossen, Florian (dir.). "Tar Baby." *Deutschland 86*. Amazon Prime. October 19, 2018.

Daniere, Elisabeth. "Französischer Rock: Käske ssäh???" *Sounds*. February 1979.

Daniere, Elisabeth. "Französischer Rock: Käske ssäh??? Teil 2 · Lyon Roque." *Sounds*. March 1979.

Diederichsen, Diedrich. "Ideologien, Identitäten, Irrwege?" SOUNDS Diskurs. *Sounds*. January 1980.

Diederichsen, Diedrich. "Untergrund und Unternehmer (Teil 2)." *Sounds*. November 1980.

Dies & Das. *Sounds*. August 1979.

Esch, Rüdiger. *Electri_city: The Düsseldorf School of Electronic Music*. London: Omnibus Press, 2016.

Evans, Jennifer V. *Life among the Ruins: Cityscape and Sexuality in Cold War Berlin*. England: Palgrave Macmillan, 2011.

"Ergebnisse National." *Sounds*. March 1979.

Fadele, Dele. "Einstürzende Neubauten: A Berlin of the Mind." *New Musical Express*. September 19, 1987.

Fessy, Emmanuel. "In East Berlin, Saturday Night Fever is Over Food, Not Disco." *The Hartford Courant*. September 3, 1981, D12.

Flint, Sunshine. "The Club Scene, on the Edge." *New York Times*. December 12, 2004, TR4.

Fukuyama, Francis. "The End of History?" *The National Interest*. Summer 1989.

Giersdorf, Jens Richard. *The Body of the People: East German Dance since 1945*. Madison: University of Wisconsin Press, 2013.

Goldstein, Patrick. "Pop Eye: In Germany, It's Agitrock." *Los Angeles Times*. October 30, 1983, U84.

Gottstein, Klaus. "The Debate on the SDI in the Federal Republic of Germany." In *Strategic Defenses and the Future of the Arms Race: A Pugwash Symposium*. Edited by John Holdren and Joseph Rotblat, 151–61. London: Macmillan, 1987.

Graf, Franziska D. "Markus KUGELBLITZE UND RAKETEN CBS 85 732." *Sounds*. June 1982.

Gröfaz and Goldmann. "Pamphlet." *Sounds*. July 1982.

Haddon, Mimi. *What Is Post-Punk?: Genre and Identity in Avant-Garde Popular Music, 1977–82*. Ann Arbor: University of Michigan Press, 2020.

Hilsberg, Alfred. "Aus grauer Städte Mauern (Teil 2): Dicke Titten und Avantgarde." *Sounds*. November 1979.

Hilsberg, Alfred. "Aus grauer Städte Mauern (Teil 3): Macher? Macht? Moneten?" *Sounds*. December 1979.

Hilsberg, Alfred. "Neue deutsche Welle; Aus grauer Städte Mauern." *Sounds*. October 1979.

Hoffmann, Josef. "Das moderne Ich: Ich-Strukturen und neue Musik." *Sounds*. September 1980.

Jacobs, Werner. *Sounds*. March 1981.

Jäger, Christian. "Ripples on a Bath of Steel—The Two Stages of *Neue Deutsche Welle* (NDW)." In *German Pop Music: A Compilation*. Edited by Uwe Schütte, 111–29. Berlin: Walter de Gruyter GmbH, 2017.

Janick, Elizabeth. *Recomposing German Music: Politics and Musical Tradition in Cold War Berlin*. Leiden: Brill, 2005.

"Joachim Witt reagiert auf 'Goldener Reiter.'" *DIFFUS*. October 5, 2022. https://www.youtube.com/watch?v=Ny3S6yX78kQ.

Jordan, Günter. *Einmal in der Woche schrein*. German Democratic Republic: DEFA-Studio für Dokumentarfilme, 1982.

Kim, Ji-Hun. "The Relationship between Berlin Club Culture and Contemporary Art." Red Bull Music Academy. https://daily .redbullmusicacademy.com/2018/08/berlin-club-culture-and -art.

Kim, Uh-Young. "Skandal-Rap: Fler und Er." *Spiegel*. May 23, 2005. https://www.spiegel.de/kultur/musik/skandal-rap-fler-und-er -a-356560.html.

Kopf, Biba. "Nena: The Girl From C&A." *New Musical Express*. May 5, 1984.

Krige, John, Angelina Long Callahan, and Ashok Maharaj. *NASA in the World: Fifty Years of International Collaboration in Space*. New York: Palgrave Macmillan, 2013.

Kröher, Michael O. R. "Die Doraus BLUMEN UND NARZISSEN Ata Tak WR 12." *Sounds*. March 1982.

Kröher, Michael O. R. "Joachim Witt: Keine Kuhhändel." *Sounds*. April, 1981.

Kröher, Michael O. R. "Untergrund und Unternehmer (Teil 1)." *Sounds*. September 1980.

Kröher, Michael O. R. "Untergrund und Unternehmer Teil 3 und Schluß." *Sounds*. December 1980.

Lauer, Marco. "Falco: Auf der Flucht vor der Banalität." *Stern*. February 6, 2008. https://www.stern.de/kultur/musik/falco-auf -der-flucht-vor-der-banalitaet-3219086.html.

Lutz, Hartmut, Florentine Strzelczyk, and Renae Watchman (eds.). *Indianthusiasm: Indigenous Responses*. Waterloo: Wilfrid Laurier University Press, 2020.

Madders, Kevin. *A New Force at a New Frontier: Europe's Development in the Space Field in the Light of its Main Actors, Policies, Law, and Activities from its Beginnings up to the Present*. Cambridge: Cambridge University Press, 1997.

Mazierska, Ewa. *Falco and Beyond: Neo Nothing Post of All.* Sheffield: Equinox, 2013.

Mazierska, Ewa. *Popular Viennese Electronic Music, 1990–2015: A Cultural History.* London: Routledge, 2019.

Mazierska, Ewa. "Tourism and Heterotopia in Falco's Songs." In *Relocating Popular Music.* Edited by Mazierska and Georgina Gregory, 167–85. New York: Palgrave MacMillan, 2015.

Mehl, Bernd. "Leserbriefe." *Sounds.* January 1980.

Morgan, Jeffrey. "Siouxsie and the Banshees: A Kiss in the Dreamhouse (Polydor)." Unpublished, 1982. Rock's Backpages Archive.

Morrison, John. "Kraftwerk and Black America: A Musical Dialogue." *The Wire.* May 2020. https://www.thewire.co.uk/in writing/essays/kraftwerk-john-morrison.

Mueuler, Christof. *Das ZickZack Prinzip: Alfred Hilsberg—Ein Leben für den Underground.* Munich: Wilhelm Heyne Verlag, 2016.

Mütter, Bernd. "*Per Media Ad Astra?* Outer Space in West Germany's Media, 1957-87." In *Imagining Outer Space: European Astroculture in the Twentieth Century.* Edited by Alexander C. T. Geppert, 165–86. London: Palgrave Macmillan, 2012.

Neuestes Deutschland. *Sounds.* July 1981.

P., Kid. "Die Wahrheit über Hamburg!" *Sounds.* May 1985.

Pareles, John. "Still Partying in the Ruins." *New York Times.* November 23, 2014, TR1.

"Poll '81." *Sounds.* February 1981.

"Popmusik: So gräßlich häßlich." *Der Spiegel*, v. 35, August 29, 1983.

"Quadripartite Agreement of September 3, 1971." In *The Berlin Settlement: The Quadripartite Agreement on Berlin and the Supplementary Arrangements*, 7–24. Wiesbaden: Press and

Information Office of the Government of the Federal Republic of Germany, 1972.

Reinhard, Kunert. "Dub." *Sounds*. July 1980.

Reinhard, Kunert. "Dub Dub Dub Dub." *Sounds*. June 1980.

Reiss, Edward. *The Strategic Defense Initiative*. Cambridge Studies in International Relations. Cambridge: Cambridge University Press, 1992.

Reynolds, Simon. *Retromania: Pop Culture's Addiction to Its Own Past*. New York: Farrar, Straus, and Giroux, 2011.

Riegel, Richard. "Nena: 99 Luftballons (Epic)." *Creem*. June 1984.

Robb, David. "Censorship, Dissent and the Metaphorical Language of GDR Rock." In *Popular Music in Eastern Europe: Breaking the Cold War Paradigm*. Edited by Ewa Mazierska, 109–28. London: Palgrave Macmillan, 2006.

Schneider, Pia. "NNDW-Sounds aus der Pfalz: Nils Keppel veröffentlicht '222.'" *DIFFUS*. https://diffusmag.de/p/nndw -sounds-aus-der-pfalz-nils-keppel-veroeffentlicht-222/#.

Schober, Ingeborg. "Genug Energie fürs Jahr 2000: La Düsseldorfs Neu~es Kraftwerk." *Sounds*. April 1979.

Seffcheque, Xao. "Joachim Witt: SILBERBLICK, WEA 58.231." Platten. *Sounds*. January 1981.

Shahan, Cyrus. "Fehlfarben and German Punk: The Making of 'No Future.'" In *German Pop Music: A Compilation*. Edited by Uwe Schütte, 131–50. Berlin: Walter de Gruyter GmbH, 2017.

"Shirin David: Zoff mit Kraftwerk wegen Sample." *Laut*. January 11, 2023. https://www.laut.de/News/Shirin-David-Zoff-mit -Kraftwerk-wegen-Sample--11-01-2023-19363.

Shukaitis, Stevphen. "Space is the (Non)place: Martians, Marxists, and the Outer Space of the Radical Imagination." In *Space Travel and Culture: From Apollo to Space Tourism*. Edited by David Bell and Martin Parker, 98–113. Malden: Wiley-Blackwell, 2009.

Smith, Russell. "Berghain and the Cult of Exclusivity." *Toronto: The Globe and Mail*. August 22, 2014, L2.

Steiner, Roland. *Unsere Kinder*. German Democratic Republic: DEFA-Studio für Dokumentarfilme, 1989.

Stender, Joachim. "Musik zwischen Anpassung und und Überwindung." SOUNDS Diskurs. *Sounds*. November, 1980.

Stubbs, David. *Future Days: Krautrock and the Building of Modern Germany*. London: Faber and Faber, 2014.

Sweet, Denis M. "A Literature of 'Truth': Writing by Gay Men in East Germany." *Studies in 20th Century Literature*, 22, iss. 1 (1998): 205–25.

Sweeting, Adam. "Fehlfarben: Before the Deluge." *Melody Maker*. July 31, 1982.

Taylor, Frederick. *The Berlin Wall: A World Divided, 1961–1989*. New York: HarperCollins, 2006.

The Associated Press. "Warner and Polygram Drop Proposed Merger." *New York Times*. November 7, 1984, 1.

Vaudeville, Jill. "Avantgarde? Scheissegal!" Sounds DISKURS. *Sounds*. April 1981.

Vaudeville, Jill. "Zwei und zwei sind nicht mehr vier—alle Mauern stürzen ein." *Sounds*. May 1980.

Walter, Klaus. "A Guide to Neue Deutsche Welle." *Red Bull Music Academy*. September 3, 2013. https://daily .redbullmusicacademy.com/2013/09/neue-deutsche-welle -feature.

Witter, Simon. "Brahms, Liszt and… Falco?" *New Music Express*. 1986.

"Gibt es noch unabhängige Neue Musik?" *Sounds*. May 1982.